IF EXPERIENCE IS SUCH A GOOD TEACHER

Why Do I Keep Repeating the Course?

◆

J. ELLSWORTH KALAS

DIMENSIONS

FOR LIVING

NASHVILLE

IF EXPERIENCE IS SUCH A GOOD TEACHER,
WHY DO I KEEP REPEATING THE COURSE?

Copyright © 2001, 1994 by Dimensions for Living

Study Guide prepared by John Schroeder

This book is printed on acid-free paper.

Library of Congress Cataloging-in-Publication Data

Kalas, J. Ellsworth, 1923–
    If experience is such a good teacher, why do I keep repeating the course? / J. Ellsworth Kalas.
        p.   cm.
* ISBN 0-687-092698 (pbk.: alk. paper)
        1. Conduct of Life.   2. Experience.   3. Wisdom—Religious aspects—Christianity.
    I. Title.
BJ1595.K29   1994
170'.44—dc20   93-44454
                                                                                          CIP
ISBN 13: 978-0-687-09269-7

"Last Act" by Frederick M. Hinshaw (p. 62) is used by permission of THE ROTARIAN.

"Outwitted" by Edwin Markham (p. 112) is used by permission of the Markham Archives, Wagner College, Staten Island, N.Y.

Scripture quotations, unless otherwise noted, are from the New Revised Standard Version Bible, copyright © 1989 by the Division of Christian Education of the National Council of the Churches of Christ in the USA. Used by permission.

Those noted RSV are from the Revised Standard Version of the Bible, copyright © 1946, 1952, 1971 by the Division of Christian Education of the National Council of the Churches of Christ in the USA. Used by permission.

07 08 09 10 11 — 13 12 11 10 9

MANUFACTURED IN THE UNITED STATES OF AMERICA

CONTENTS

INTRODUCTION TO A
REMARKABLE FACULTY

(THEY ALL HOLD TENURE)

We've all heard that Experience is the best teacher, but many of us have been in its classes long enough to know that its reputation is overrated. If Experience was so effective, we'd all be practicing geniuses by middle age, because all of us get equal time in its care.

It seems true, though, that Experience is the most popular of all schools—at least, if one is to judge from the size of class enrollment. But even that statement should be qualified, because many who take courses in Experience don't really choose to do so, they just fall into the sessions as if the classes were required. Still more don't necessarily learn anything in the courses they take. No matter how many years they sit under the instruction of Experience, they never seem to give it the kind of attention that makes learning possible. If ever there were a school that could feel discouraged by results, it would be this most vaunted of institutions: Experience.

So do we learn anything at all in the School of Experience? I think of the young Talmudic scholar who, having just completed his first book and wanting to be sure it got a good audience, begged a learned rabbi for a testimonial. The rabbi answered gently, "My son, you must face the stern realities. If you wish to be a writer of learned books, you must be resigned to peddle your work from house to house like a vendor of pots and pans and suffer hunger until you are forty."

"And what will happen when I'm forty?" the young scholar asked hopefully.

The rabbi smiled. "By the time you are forty, you will be used to it."

In case that seems to be the end of it all, I'd like to give the School of Experience a little help. Since all of us go to the school, want to or not, and since all of us deal with its faculty, wittingly or unwittingly, the point is to make each session profitable.

Part of the secret is to realize that Experience is not a single teacher, but an entire faculty. It is so diverse a faculty that what succeeds in one course may solicit disaster in another. I can't hope to introduce you to all those who teach under Experience's banner; as a matter of fact, I haven't yet met all of them. But let me give you an idea of what is in store.

We're inclined to think of Experience as a tough curriculum, so you may be surprised to find such teachers as Love, Success, and Friendship on the faculty. Frankly, I don't know why we don't give them more attention, because there's no reason why we can't learn from life's kindliness as well as from its more severe experiences. If we would give more attention to what Success teaches, we might skip some of the courses offered by Defeat.

And speaking of skipping courses, one of the finest teachers is often one of the most underrated. I'm speaking of People. If we will learn from the experience of other people, we can avoid some courses for ourselves. But here's the irony: we generally recognize the value of courses taught by people after we have gone through the same material. How often have you said, "I should have known better. After all, my mother told me any number of times that . . ."?

You won't be surprised to find Sorrow on this faculty, and also Pain, Loneliness, and Defeat, which I have already mentioned. And then there's Regret. Some of us spend years of our lives in the class of Regret, without ever seeming to learn a thing. We re-enroll each morning, and cram for its courses each night—in spite of the fact that Regret is an unpleasant teacher.

Don't be surprised to find Death on the faculty. After all, life would be exceedingly unfair if it didn't give us a chance to cram for an exam that is inevitable. You can learn much from Death before you actually face it. And while I wish we all could avoid Sin (moralist that I am!), I have to admit there's much to be learned from Sin. Sin is such a poor teacher, however, that most people don't learn from it. Those who learn the most from Sin are the saints, those whom the unknowing think are naive about Sin.

Then there are Enemies. No matter how you try, you're sure to have some. Try, therefore, to learn from them. It will frustrate them to no end if you do.

Sometimes the teachers in the School of Experience give us lessons that will benefit us in dealing with other aspects of life, while sometimes the secret is to learn enough so that we never again need to face that particular faculty member. In other instances (Sorrow, for example), we need to cut back on the time we spend in the course. The aim is not so much to learn from the class itself as to be prepared to deal with the experience when it comes.

I've drawn my "research" for this book from saints and sages, but also from rogues; some people's major contribution to life is to show us how *not* to live! Although the Bible is my major source, one of the Bible's marks of inspiration is the way it is confirmed by the accumulation of human experience; and I've relied upon many other sources. Included are stories and quotes from well-known figures, but also from people of whom you've never heard, who have somewhere crossed my path. And of course from time to time I dare to reflect on my own experiences—sometimes with a measure of pain.

Harvard students used to receive an unofficial but very candid guide to the institution; it told so much more than the college's official publications! This little book is meant, in a very modest way, to serve as such a guide to the School of Experience. I hope its pages will equip you to make the most of those learning possibilities that are open to—and sometimes forced upon—every human being.

J. Ellsworth Kalas

1

LONELINESS IS A PRIVATE TUTOR . . .

WHERE ELSE CAN YOU GET SUCH PERSONAL ATTENTION?

Thomas Wolfe was one of the finest novelists of this century. *Look Homeward, Angel* is a staple in most college contemporary literature courses, and *You Can't Go Home Again* has become a phrase in our common speech.

Wolfe was also a lonely man. He once thought that loneliness was something suffered especially, perhaps even uniquely, by the young, so he wrote an essay titled "On Loneliness at Twenty-Three." For a time he thought of himself as perhaps the loneliest person who ever lived. But gradually he came to a broader conclusion. Loneliness, he said, "far from being a rare and curious phenomenon . . . is the central and inevitable fact of human existence" (Thomas Wolfe, "God's Lonely Man," in *The Spirit of Man*, ed. Whit Burnett, 20).

Wolfe's later conclusion is almost surely right. Being human means having the capacity to be lonely; loneliness is part of what it means to be human. The only way to be entirely free of loneliness would be to become utterly indifferent to human beings and even to animals; and, especially, to be oblivious to God and the eternal. But if we had no feelings for people, for animals, or for God, we could hardly be called human. To be human is to be susceptible to loneliness.

We shouldn't be surprised, then, that loneliness is no respecter of age. Almost a generation ago a British study concluded that persons between the ages of thirty and fifty are the most prone to loneliness. This loneliness probably reflects the transitional pain of middle age. At that point in life, we begin to recognize that some of our dreams will never come true. The age varies with the dream, of course. For those whose dreams are built on physical attractiveness, the thirties can be threatening. Career dreams are usually tested just a little later, along with romance and fantasy. Then loneliness becomes a greater issue because at middle age we find it hard to confide our dreams to others, as we did when we were younger—especially in their broken state. And with that, a unique loneliness sets in.

A multitude of older people would argue that the loneliness of old age is far worse. Many of one's peers have died and infirmities bring on more isolation, both physical and social. I will never forget an octogenarian in a church I once served as pastor. He was bedfast and very hard of hearing. "But the loneliness is the worst," he told me on nearly every pastoral call. "The loneliness is the worst."

If the loneliness of age is painful, what about the loneliness of childhood? Is anything more painful than being shut out of the circle of play, or is anyone lonelier than the child at the edge of the playground? And how can one imagine the loneliness of the abused or rejected child? Some psychologists say that one of the main reasons infants cry during the first three months of life is loneliness. Since they so often stop crying when they are cuddled, it seems likely that their cries are not from physical pain but from loneliness, from the need to be embraced. If that be so, one wonders what happens to a tiny human being when the cry of loneliness is ignored, or perhaps even punished.

MODERN LIFE ACCENTUATES LONELINESS

Modern life blesses us in many ways, but it may only increase our loneliness. The popular long-distance telephone slogan "Reach out and touch someone" is a tacit admission of our problem and our need. Mother Teresa, who has seen the worst of the world's poverty, says that loneliness is the greatest poverty in the United States. Evangelist Vance Havner liked to point out that no generation has had more amusements and entertainment than modern Americans, but that there have never been more lonely people.

Technology itself may be our enemy. Television has all but eliminated conversation in many families, except for a shouted, "Don't change that channel!" Someone has argued rather persuasively that the dishwasher —a generally wonderful invention—has robbed homes of one of the guaranteed visiting periods. A

15

parent washed, a child rinsed, and another child dried—and perhaps still another put the dishes in the cupboard. It was a regular, built-in time for getting together, and inevitably, for talking.

We used to talk with a bank teller, but now we bank with a plastic card in a machine. The service station attendant was once someone who knew not only the peculiarities of our automobile, but also the names of our family members; now we pump our own gasoline and pay at a pump-side credit card machine or at a window to someone who often says not a word. More and more service industries are peopled by part-time employees, so that we rarely see the same checkout clerk or table server on consecutive visits to a place of business. We now realize that these "lost" relationships, which we may have thought were only incidental and routine, were part of the significant fabric of community. Without them, loneliness is far more threatening. No wonder some older people come to think of soap opera characters as real people—in some peculiar, pathetic sense, the best friends they have!

PEOPLE NEED PEOPLE

No amount of technology or creature comfort can take the place of people. It has always been so. The Genesis story makes that clear in the most poignant fashion. The story pictures a man, Adam, alone in an idyllic setting, an unspoiled creation of exquisite beauty. This was indeed a Camelot, with perfect climate, natural beauty, and absolute security. Adam must have enjoyed easy communication with God.

Nevertheless, something was missing. So looking at Adam, God said, "It is not good that he should be alone" (Gen. 2:18, paraphrase). A human being is meant to commune, to touch, to be touched. God answered this need at first with the animals. They were good, but not adequate. They couldn't enter into the depth of relationship that human beings need. For our capacity, you see, is also our necessity. Because we have this ability to commune, we are unfulfilled if we do not commune. So God gave Adam someone just like himself, only remarkably different: Eve. Adam described her as bone of his bone and flesh of his flesh, the stuff of his very being. Yet she was different enough that they complemented, rather than simply duplicated, each other.

We know this story is true—even though there are no historical artifacts to substantiate it—not only because it is in the Bible, but also because it is so true to our human experience. We human beings are social creatures. We are singular enough that we need some solitude, but incomplete enough and similar enough that we need one another.

SIN AND LONELINESS

As Genesis portrays it, if things had remained perfect, we might never again have known loneliness. If you and I always understood one another, and if we always tried, unfailingly, to fulfill one another's needs, we probably would never be lonely. But our self-centeredness gets in the way of such perfect communication; we are often too preoccupied to hear the other

17

person really well, and our own insecurities prevent our being as honest as we should.

"Besides," someone answers, "we would still be lonely when we're separated from one another." Perhaps not, if it were not for the prospect of death. If sin and death hadn't entered our human story, other forms of separation would carry no real threat. Separation would have no ultimate point of reference, and thus no real sting, if death were not such an ever-present reality. We don't realize the extent to which death informs and poisons all our other experiences of life. If our temporary separations were not colored by the ultimate prospect of deathly separation, they would affect our relationships only as part of a kind of social inspiration-expiration cycle.

Loneliness is the point of intersection between our divine roots and our sinful inclinations. We crave one another because we were made with a capacity for communion, but we never quite fulfill one another because sin complicates our relationships and dulls our communication. A romantic song says, "You have made my life complete," but that's too much to ask of another human being. Our humanness gets in the way of such completeness.

LONELINESS CAN BRING CREATIVITY AND SENSITIVITY

Loneliness is one of life's inevitable teachers, but what does it have to offer? Some people spend a large part of their lives under the tutelage of loneliness, often to their great pain. Since we must deal with it, what can we learn? The possibilities in the classroom of Loneliness are almost endless, but two seem to stand out from the rest.

First, loneliness can lead to creativity. I think, for instance, of the novelist Thomas Wolfe. He wrote with such power and insight partly because he was lonely, and in his loneliness he reflected on the human condition with a sensitivity that he never would have owned if it were not for his loneliness. A creative writing teacher used to tell his classes that he could never be a great novelist because he was too happily married! He was saying, in effect, that he had not been taught by loneliness. In his introduction to *Cat on a Hot Tin Roof,* Tennessee Williams, one of the greatest playwrights of this century, told of the role of loneliness in writing. I wonder how many of the world's great creative works never would have been created if it had not been for the loneliness that drove the artist, the composer, the writer. Creativity is so often born and nurtured in lonely places.

Loneliness also can make us more sensitive to other people. If you have experienced the loneliness of bereavement, you probably will have more heart for someone who has just lost a loved one. If you can remember how you felt when you were separated from the first girl or boy you ever loved, you won't be quite so likely to mutter "puppy love" when you see a teenager walking about in a lonely daze. Some of the best and kindest listeners I've ever known have been lonely people. They have experienced the anguish of inner aloneness and are therefore ready to listen to someone else.

LONELINESS IS ONLY AS GOOD AS ITS STUDENTS

Unfortunately, loneliness doesn't work its benefits automatically; it is not a foolproof teacher. If loneliness makes some people sensitive listeners, it just as surely makes others tedious and unceasingly talkative. Some lonely people become bitter toward the whole human race. Some drink themselves into oblivion. Some become insensitive to others because they are so absorbed with their own pain. Loneliness, like every other teacher in the School of Experience, can teach only those who are willing to learn. And if we're willing to learn, one of the most significant lessons will be a deeper insight into ourselves.

When we become lonely for some person in particular, or for communion in general, we realize that we are not completely self-sufficient. Sometimes we suppress our loneliness, or at least any expression of it, because we don't want to make such a concession to the rest of the human race. But when we suppress this need, we kill a part of ourselves, and we are smaller and poorer for it. A popular song that seems to have become what musicians call "a standard," says, "People who need people are the luckiest people in the world." Actually, *all* people need people, though perhaps in different measure and in different ways. But the experiences of life, including its disappointments and rejections, cause some people to isolate themselves from others. The lucky ones are those who are willing to pay the price of relationships.

On the other hand, loneliness can also teach us that we should not lay on others too much of a burden for

20

our happiness. We dare not depend on any single individual for our fulfillment; it isn't fair to that person, and it inevitably leads to an experience of devastation. Much of our poetry, novels, and plays glory in portraying the kind of love or friendship that becomes the focus of all of life. Such a theme makes beautiful poetry, and even more so when it is set to music, but it doesn't *live* very well. We lay an impossible burden on another human when we make our happiness contingent upon their devotion and unfailing availability. Loneliness should teach us to have a broader focus, for the sake of the other person and for our own emotional survival.

I spent more than twenty years of my life, beginning sometime in my teens and continuing until age forty, fighting recurrent bouts of loneliness. It was not the natural loneliness that is associated with the nearness or distance of my family and friends, but a loneliness that could bring struggle on even the loveliest of days and sometimes with those most cherished near at hand.

My deliverance came through a religious experience, and I am eternally grateful for it. But I try never to forget some things I learned through those years of recurring, baffling loneliness. When loneliness seemed a harsh and heartless teacher, I came to have deeper sympathy for the human race. I learned to look for the pain in other people's eyes. I concluded that loneliness may well be the oldest human pain, older perhaps than Eden. In a sense, it may be the root human illness, tied as it is to our experience of sin. At the very least, it is always a complicating illness. I'm sure that my experience with loneliness has colored my writing and speaking. I never write for an audience or speak to a group without thinking—*There are lonely people out there.* Sometimes, human as I am, I forget it during the course of a day's run, but never for long. Loneliness taught me too well.

LONELINESS AND GOD

Above all, loneliness should teach us to find a better friendship with God. The ultimate relationship for us human beings—beyond nature, beyond pets, beyond other human beings—is our tie with the eternal. This body and its touch will someday go, but the part of us that reaches out toward God will endure forever. We shouldn't expect God to make other humans unnecessary—the Genesis story of Adam and Eve proves otherwise—but a better relationship with God deals with the eternal issues of loneliness and equips us to enter more effectively into our human relationships.

William Cowper, the eighteenth-century poet, struggled with exceeding loneliness through much of his life, to the point of great depression. Through it all, he drew close to God. He left us with several lasting hymns, one of which includes these words:

> Ye fearful saints, fresh courage take;
> The clouds you so much dread
> Are big with mercy, and shall break
> In blessings on your head.

I doubt that Cowper ever would have written with such faith and insight if he had not struggled with loneliness and found a deeper friendship with God.

Norman Vincent Peale was passing through LaGuardia Airport several years ago en route to a speaking engagement. The agent, who knew him, also knew that Mrs. Peale often traveled with him. He said to Dr. Peale, "Traveling alone today, I see." "Yes," Dr. Peale answered, "I am traveling alone."

But as Dr. Peale moved away from the check-in counter, the man called after him, "You never travel alone." And Dr. Peale replied, "Nor do you."

None of us needs to make this journey alone. There is One who will go with us everywhere, even into the world to come. Loneliness should teach us to make *that* friendship strong and continuous. So strong that we will be able to affirm the words of the old prayer meeting hymn: "On life's pathway, I am never lonely." But if at times we become lonely, we can make the lonely place into a blessed classroom.

2

FRIENDSHIP IS THE LOVELIEST TEACHER . . .

SO LOVELY, YOU CAN EASILY MISS THE LESSONS

In the years I spent as a student, I had several teachers who were so pleasant that the classes were a sheer delight. These instructors always created an air of excitement about the material, and they expressed an obvious love for the students. It was all so pleasurable that at times I hardly realized how much I was learning.

Friendship is that kind of teacher. The touch is usually gentle, the style inobtrusive. Even when the lessons are difficult, we feel the embrace of good will. Of course, friendship is not infallible, since it involves human beings at both the giving and receiving ends. But perhaps no teacher in the School of Experience treats its students so kindly.

The ancient wise man said:

> There are friends who pretend to be
> friends,

> but there is a friend who sticks closer
> than a brother.
> (Prov. 18:24 RSV)

I wish I knew the circumstances in which those words were written. Even without having specific details, it's easy to speculate that this person had gone through some particular human struggle in which help was desperately needed and in which likely sources may have failed. But all along the way, there was a *friend*. Perhaps there were several. Not all of them were of the same quality, but each was appropriate to the varying fortunes of life and wondrous enough to make the writer say, "There is a friend who sticks closer than a brother."

FRIENDSHIP HAS ITS RISKS

But in the same breath there is a warning. Friendship has its risks. This person who testified that a friend can be priceless also acknowledged that there are those "who pretend to be friends." There are counterfeits in friendship. That shouldn't surprise us, because anything as valuable as friendship is sure to encourage counterfeiting. Some people feign friendship only for the profit it brings; in their minds, "profit" is part of the very definition of friendship. They see it as little more than a technique to be employed in the pursuit of success. Others maintain a shallow level of friendship because they are essentially shallow people, picking up friendships easily and dropping them just as easily.

Even the best and truest friends are human, and they can disappoint us because of the natural boundaries of humanness—just as we can disappoint them. People

26

have troubles of their own, and when we expect them to invest too much emotional energy in our concerns, we're likely to be hurt.

So make up your mind, as you pursue friendship, that you may be disappointed, perhaps even disillusioned. At the same time, remind yourself that you may—even unknowingly—disappoint or disillusion someone else. Sometimes we're unrealistic in our expectations of others, and they in turn may expect too much of us. Reconcile yourself to the fact that friendship entails risk. Anything of so much value must have its hazards.

FRIENDSHIP HAS MANY FACES

Friendship comes in various shapes and sizes. Some friendships last for only a few years, yet for that time they are warm and significant. Friends may even be lost from the Christmas card list, yet the mention of their names will evoke a complex array of affectionate memories. Other friendships are the product of a limited common interest. I hear some say, "He's my fishing buddy," or "She's a golf friend." I don't happen to fish or golf, but I understand what they mean. I have such an identification for some service club friends from Rotary. These may not be profound friendships, yet they contribute to the wondrous fabric of life, its network of meaning.

There are also those who are friends-in-passing. I'm thinking of Bill, to whom I took my dry cleaning for years, and Stan, from whom I bought suits. With their retirement or death, my world grew measurably smaller. I didn't need John Donne to tell me that my life had been diminished. On the surface, our relationship might be classified as incidental or superficial, yet a bond of trust was there; these men were part of the wholeness of my life. We enjoyed a code of predictable repartee; each of us made the other smile and feel better. We were friends.

Then there are those friends of whom the wise man wrote: friends who stick closer than a brother. If, as tradition says, this proverb was written by King Solomon, I venture he learned it from his father, David, and his father's friendship with Jonathan. When David was a rustic shepherd boy, he was brought to King Saul's palace. In time, Saul became insanely jealous of the young man and tried repeatedly to kill him. Only one person dared to identify publicly with David—Saul's son, Jonathan. And Jonathan did so even though he recognized that David would someday become king, a position that was Jonathan's by inheritance. Jonathan's quality of friendship was so unspoiled that he would sacrifice his own dreams and put his life in peril in order to be a friend to David.

Friends of that quality prove themselves at the two extremities of life, notable success and failure. Only very special people weep when we weep and rejoice when we rejoice. An older friend once asked me of a certain professional colleague, "Do you think he is really your friend?" I answered, "We enjoy one another's company, but I don't think he would feel bad if I failed." Years later, however, when I had to cope with a personal failure, this man proved to be a loyal friend. I had sold him short. I didn't fully realize the degree of his caring.

THE PECULIAR CHEMISTRY OF FRIENDSHIP

The story of David and Jonathan also shows how mysterious a relationship friendship can be. On the surface, those two young men would seem to have had little in common. David was a shepherd by heritage, at home in the hills outside Bethlehem, while Jonathan grew up in a king's palace, enjoying all the benefits of a royal family. What did they have in common? Samuel Johnson, who knew a good deal about friendship, once said, "Friendship is seldom lasting but between equals, or where the superiority on one side is reduced by some equivalent advantage on the other" (*The Rambler*). I recognize Johnson's point, yet I marvel at the strange patterns of friendship. I think of several close friends and wonder how we found each other! On the other hand, I think of a number of persons who I thought would make ideal friends; it seemed we had so much in common. Yet friendship never developed in these instances beyond the most casual level. The chemistry of good friendship is very hard to analyze.

There's much to be said for seeking friendships that leap the usual boundaries of life. When I was younger, some of my best relationships came with those a generation or two removed from me. We were not peers, but that didn't prevent our being friends. I am more grateful than I can say for those older persons who were patient enough to overlook my immaturity and become my friends. As I grow older, I hope I will remain sensitive to the possibility of friendships with some who are much younger than I am.

The same point can also be made regarding social, economic, and educational differences. When I was a pastor in a university community, I was struck by the number of times a very real friendship developed between professors and graduate students. They were often at opposite ends of their careers, and unequal in economic and social status. Yet somehow they found a common ground of mutual respect. I've also seen substantial friendships that bridged great economic differences, in which two parties or two couples cherished each other for qualities of character and mutual commitments, regardless of their disparate bank balances.

All of us need the stimulation and broadening that come from relationships with those who are different from ourselves; and we need to give something of ourselves to others who may at first be difficult to relate to. If we restrict our friendships to those who are nearly identical to us in education, life-style, and outlook, we will limit the effectiveness of friendship in teaching us.

FRIENDSHIP TEACHES NEW PRIORITIES

Secular society tells us to look at the bottom line, which generally means, "What's in it for me?" Friendship teaches us that there is more to life than can be measured in such self-centered ways. Now this may sound contradictory. I've been insisting that friendship is a great teacher, benefiting us in numerous ways, which seems to suggest that friendship itself is something to be used. Someone has said, however, that the only kind of selfishness that works is unselfishness. So it is with friendship. The moment we make it utilitarian, it ceases to be friendship. Friendship needs no other justification than itself; it cannot be asked to "pay."

30

Friendship teaches us that people have worth without any measurable return; we will be friends simply because it is right to be friendly.

For five years I was privileged to be pastor to a retired pastor and his spouse. They had accumulated friends in nearly every part of the world, and even in retirement they maintained a voluminous correspondence. A pragmatist might say that they had quite enough friends, and that they could now settle down, in their later years, to enjoy what they had.

Their attitude was quite the opposite. Each Sunday morning they circulated throughout the church, shaking hands with people, particularly seeking out people they didn't know. Many Sundays they would find a university student or some other young person and invite them to brunch that very day—none of this "we must get together sometime." In a sense, they didn't need more friends, but they believed in friendship; so they gave it abundantly to others, especially to some who might be in short supply.

Henry Adams said, "One friend in a lifetime is much; two are many; three are hardly possible" (*The Education of Henry Adams*, 20). If one judges friendship only at the level of those who "stick closer than a sibling," Adams might be right. But friendship has many levels, and friendship would teach us to have respect for all its levels and to recognize that there is more to life than what can be measured by any so-called bottom line. Besides, if we don't keep cultivating friendships, we may find ourselves declaring social bankruptcy. There is so much movement in our society that friends can soon be scattered from one coast to the other; then, as time goes by, death makes its inroads. If we don't continue to make deposits in the bank of relationships, we someday may find that old friends are gone and we have no one to take their place.

LIFE IS RICHEST AS WE GIVE TO RELATIONSHIPS

For many years I belonged to a small interfaith clergy group that met half a dozen times a year to read and discuss a paper, then enjoy dinner together. Near the end of one of those meals, someone said rather pensively, "You know, life doesn't get much better than this—having good food with good friends." Food eaten in friendship is more than food; its flavor is sharpened by conversation and caring. Especially *caring*. I speak not simply of those times when the world is caving in, but of the times when caring shows itself in thoughtful listening and appreciative noticing. Life is made very rich when we give ourselves to someone. True friendship teaches us that.

William Barclay tells of a November day when he saw a notice on a bulletin board of the London Central YMCA saying that Basil Oliver had died and that the funeral was to be that day, with a memorial service the following week. By the nature of the bulletin, Barclay said, you would have thought Oliver was a very important person—and in a sense, you would have been right, for everyone who had anything to do with the Central YMCA in London knew of him.

Basil Oliver was eighty-five years old when he died. More than thirty years before, sometime after the death

32

of his wife, he had moved to London and had rented a room at the Central YMCA. When he retired, he began helping out in every possible way—collecting letters, going out for stamps, running errands, buying Sunday papers for staff members. But more than that, he was doing all sorts of kindnesses that most people knew nothing about until after he had died and they began sharing stories.

Dr. Barclay describes Oliver as a "supremely happy man," "a supremely useful man," and "a supremely kind man." And then Barclay says, recalling that Oliver had come to the big, somewhat impersonal, city YMCA after becoming a widower: "He might have been a lonely man, but he had thousands of friends" (William Barclay, *In the Hands of God*, 11-13). By giving himself to others, Basil Oliver became rich in human relationships.

FRIENDSHIP AND GOD

In the course of leading spiritual life renewals in local churches, I'm often asked to talk with the middle and high school young people. In the course of my remarks, I inevitably talk about Harry, Roy, and Bud, church friends in my high school days. We were such good friends that we could talk about the most important things in life—namely, God and girls. In our increasingly impersonal society, we don't often have friends with whom we can discuss our divine longings and to whom we can confess our shortcomings. That's unfortunate, because we've never needed them more.

Something special happens in friendship when Christ is the focus. Jesus promised his followers that where two or three come together in his name, he will be present (Matt. 18:20). This isn't an assurance that God blesses small attendance at worship services! It is testimony to a common, extraordinary experience: when those who believe in Christ engage in faith-talk, friendship reaches its highest potential. At such times we find that as two talk, three are there; as four talk, there are five in the gathering. The particular quality of conversation may be thanksgiving, soul-searching, or confession, but the distinguishing characteristic is always the same—a sense of the Lordship of Christ, and of lives bound in friendship through him.

No doubt about it, friendship is a lovely teacher. But to learn its lessons, we have to engage ourselves with a high level of unselfishness. Friendship teaches profound lessons, such as the inexplicable devotion that endures even to the point of death, but friendship also teaches such simple lessons as daily thoughtfulness, courtesy, and kindness. To learn friendship's lessons really well, we need the gift of divine love. But even the poorest students are well rewarded. Friendship is that kind of teacher.

3

DON'T SEEK PAIN . . .

BUT IF IT COMES, EMBRACE IT

When I was in grade school, a teacher double-promoted me. She said I already knew everything that grade could offer. I was proud and excited, of course, but years later I sometimes wondered if I had missed something. Is there a gap somewhere in my education as a result of that double promotion?

I had the same feeling one day when a man said, "I've never had a sick day in my life." My first reaction was to say, "And you don't have a very good memory." But I resisted that impulse while I pondered that if the man were right, he had also missed something. Some courses in the School of Experience are omitted at great loss. They are so very nearly essential that to miss them is to leave a strategic empty spot in our character. I think that's true of the experience of pain, illness, and suffering.

Before I go further, let me make a disclaimer. I don't "believe" in sickness; I believe in health. Most of us give far too much power to illness by our negative state of mind. I don't want to increase the power of sickness by giving it more recognition than it deserves. Pain is a reality, but it is not the ultimate reality. Health is the ultimate reality, because our bodies are so constructed that they have unbelievable, built-in power to heal themselves. We ought to concentrate on the body's inclination toward health rather than its occasions of sickness.

While I'm giving disclaimers, let me remind you of another one that must be said of every course in the School of Experience. Pain can be a most instructive teacher, so that our lives may hardly be complete without encountering it; nevertheless, pain doesn't always get its lesson across. The late Bishop Fulton Sheen once said, "Pain of itself does not make us better; it is very apt to make us worse. No one was ever better simply because he had an earache" (Fulton Sheen, *The Rainbow of Sorrow,* 28). Suffering produces sainthood and character in some, but it develops hypochondria and self-centeredness in others. In this course, as the saying goes, you pay your money and you take your choice.

PAIN BECOMES A HAPPY SONG IF WE LEARN FROM IT

Some anonymous soul, centuries before Christ, learned much from pain. Whether it was a man or a woman, we do not know; the testimony is found in the longest chapter of the Bible, Psalm 119. This remarkable chapter has just one basic theme: the importance and beauty of the law of God. We learn God's law in

36

the crucible of experience. This writer recalls what pain did in his or her life:

> Before I was afflicted, I went astray;
> but now I keep thy word.
> (Ps. 119:67 RSV)

This is the confession of a good human being, whose relationship to God was a cherished part of life. Such a person would seem to be so spiritually sensitive that there would be no need for external incentives. But in truth, all of us need some prodding now and then, and so it was with this person. Taking soul-inventory, the writer realized that his or her life had somehow gone astray, and had then been brought back on track by affliction. Sickness had had a salutary effect.

The writer picks up the same theme a few lines later:

> It is good for me that I was afflicted,
> that I might learn thy statutes.
> (Ps. 119:71 RSV)

Affliction isn't usually high on our thanksgiving list, but it was for the psalmist. Realizing what might have happened to his or her soul, and how close he or she was to serious straying, the poet concludes that affliction was one of the best things that could have happened.

I'm impressed that this is not a sad song. The writer doesn't tell us how much he or she has suffered, but only that the suffering has done so much good. It isn't a recital of anguish, but a very tumult of thanksgiving.

John Greenleaf Whittier, the nineteenth-century poet, was a man of sensitive conscience. Several of his poems have found a place in many Christian hymn collections, where they help draw our souls toward God. During a serious illness, Whittier wrote, "I think sickness has a wonderful effect in fanning into life the half-extinguished conscience." The human conscience is such a fragile thing that it can easily be reduced in power and direction by the pressures of daily life. During sickness, Whittier saw his conscience reawakened to full power.

Rabbi Tanna Akiba noted that Judah's King Manasseh had been raised and taught by a very godly father, yet he persisted in evil. Then affliction came. "The only teacher that finally proved effective," Akiba said, "was affliction." Then he added, "Precious affliction!" No wonder that anonymous poet in Psalm 119 sang a song of thanksgiving for pain. Its end result, if we will learn, is joy, because it elevates the soul. But only if we let it.

PAIN IS A GREAT EQUALIZER

Years ago I knew a young preacher whose first name was Andrew but whom everyone called Slim. He was a tall, handsome, athletic man, and he believed in divine healing. He preached about it often, telling his congregations that there was no reason for anyone to be sick, because God wanted them to enjoy health. Unfortunately, in his enthusiasm he was often insensitive toward those who were sick.

One day Slim got some new personal insight. He told me about himself. "I've never been ill," he said, "and my good health made me arrogant. I haven't really

known how to sympathize with people who aren't as robust as I am. This has made my preaching mean and harsh. I haven't had much compassion." It's remarkable that he came to such insight without himself passing through the valley of physical pain. Most of us don't understand pain—or the boundaries of human weakness—until we've suffered a share of it.

Affliction is a great equalizer. It makes us all brothers and sisters in a very special way. Almost anyone who has ever shared a hospital room remembers their roommate; they have traveled together in the fellowship of suffering, and even if they never see each other again, they often feel uniquely close. This is partly because pain treats us all alike. It's easier to endure sickness in a private room than in a ward, but when you have to depend on a nurse or an aide for bedpan and bathing, it makes no difference whether you're rich or poor, learned or ignorant. And if you're accustomed to being independent, the burden may be all the harder to bear.

In 1893, shortly after Grover Cleveland had come into his second term in the presidency, it was discovered that he had cancer of the throat and jaw. National leaders feared that if his illness became public knowledge, the shaky financial condition of the country might grow into a full panic. So they arranged for a medical team to join the president on a yacht, and skilled surgeons operated as the craft rolled up the East River. "If you must have surgery," someone might say, "that's the way to have it." Perhaps. But Cleveland wrote later, "I have learned how weak the strongest man is under God's decree; and I see in a new light the necessity of doing my allotted work in the full apprehension of the coming night."

Pain is a great equalizer. Peasant or president, rich or poor, the dimensions are pretty much the same.

PAIN AFFECTS SOUL AND SPIRIT AS WELL AS BODY

I've been using several words interchangeably. I have called this teacher *pain,* but I have spoken also of illness and suffering. The terms are not by any means identical in meaning, but they are interrelated in the way in which I'm using them. They remind us that the line between physical and emotional suffering is often hard to distinguish. So it is with the origins of pain. Sometimes our physical illnesses begin with mental anguish or distress of spirit, while in other instances physical illness leads to mental distress. You and I are such finely interwoven combinations of the physical and the spiritual that we cannot touch one without affecting the other.

So while physical illness is a fact of the body, its impact on soul, mind, and emotions—those hard-to-define areas—is very significant. No wonder, then, that the ancient poet was glad to have been afflicted, because affliction brought knowledge of God's law. Did the poet mean that the experience of pain drove him or her to study the law? Or was it that suffering made the poet realize the law's importance? Or was the poet perhaps more mystical, telling us that suffering had made the law come alive in ways not sensed before?

Regardless of the poet's meaning, it is clear that pain affected every aspect of his or her being.

PAIN PUTS LIFE IN PERSPECTIVE

Affliction is particularly effective in helping us re-evaluate our priorities. When Thomas Chalmers became pastor of the church at Kilmany, Scotland in 1803, he was a young man of twenty-three with little real interest in religion. He had taken the parish primarily so that he could also teach mathematics and astronomy.

As time went by, Chalmers neglected sermon preparation and the care of his people. The church went into steady and precipitous decline. After several years he was stricken with a serious illness. For four months he was unable to leave his sick room, and for almost a year he did not preach. Slowly he came to realize that his view of Christianity as simply an ethical system was not sufficient to see him through this valley of the shadow of death. There in the lonely place of his illness he faced himself and the shallowness of his beliefs, until he experienced a dramatic religious conversion.

In the years that followed, Chalmers became the most powerful preacher in Scotland. And with it, he came to have a compelling social conscience. The finest pulpits in Scotland were available to him, but he also chose to minister to the poorest of the population in special services on a tanner's second story. A century later Lord Roseberry said of him, "An illness lifted him into a higher sphere, and he soared aloft." Illness can do that to us, because it helps us get our values in order.

41

In John Donne's most quoted devotional, he acknowledges that some might feel he is borrowing misery. If so, he says, it would be "an excusable covetousness," because "affliction is a treasure, and scarce any man hath enough of it. No one hath affliction enough that is not matured and ripened by it, and made fit for God by the affliction."

I'm not an expert in pain, but I will testify to the truth of Donne's statement. Through most of my adult life I have been blessed with extraordinary health and a body which, while not athletic, has seemed nearly indestructible. But some years ago I began to have difficulty swallowing. I tried to ignore it, because I've always reasoned that most physical problems go away in time. This one did not; instead it grew steadily worse. I intensified my pain by dealing with the matter alone, because I felt I shouldn't burden anyone with what was happening.

Eventually I went to our family doctor, and by his direction to specialists, and I learned that there would have to be surgery. It was not a malignancy (a word that seems to shadow all our thinking) but a relatively rare affliction, a diverticulum in the esophagus.

I wasn't worried about death. Not that it wasn't a prospect, for when someone is going to cut your throat, the possibilities are clear! But I felt I had already been blessed with more than fifty good years and therefore should have no complaint if I were to make my exit. I had to face, rather, the question of my calling. Only a slight error on the part of the surgeon, the least fraction of an inch, could mean I would never preach again, or that I would do so with a voice that would be a handicap rather than an asset. How much of a chance this was, I didn't know, but it was the issue I had to wrestle through in my own soul. I love to preach. It has been my calling and my passionate commitment since I was ten years old. What if I were never able to preach again?

It's difficult for those in any type of ministry to keep their work in perspective. I believe my calling is of God, but it is also a job—one for which I receive paychecks regularly. It is, therefore, a peculiar mix of divine and human, and I think we ministers can often lose the divine in the constant presence of the human.

So I asked myself what my ultimate Employer, my Lord, might have in mind for me. Suppose God was done with my preaching? As I saw it, my preaching and my creative powers were only beginning to reach their potential, but I had to remember that I am not the final arbiter. I am *God's* employee, and he can use me when and how he chooses.

I thought especially of the searching words in John Wesley's Covenant Service:

> I am no longer mine, but thine. Put me to what thou wilt, rank me with whom thou wilt; put me to doing, put me to suffering; let me be employed for thee or laid aside for thee, exalted for thee or brought low for thee; let me be full, let me be empty; let me have all things, let me have nothing . . .

One phrase stood out in particular: "Let me be employed for thee or laid aside for thee." Perhaps it was my time to be laid aside.

In those soul-searching days preceding the surgery, God's X ray pierced my thinking, cutting to the center of my very being. I asked myself anew how much of my work was for love of God and how much of it was for my personal pleasure, ambition, and benefit; and I made a special kind of peace with God. I thank God that, in the midst of a remarkably healthy life, I had days of affliction. Some mornings, when I shave, I look with awe on the scar on my throat.

The old village preacher said that sickness has its value, because when you're flat on your back, there's no place to look but *up*. With such a focus, life can take on different proportions. That's what the psalmist meant when he or she said, "It is good for me that I was afflicted." Don't court pain, but if and when it comes, embrace it. Pain can be a wondrous teacher.

4

REGRET IS A HUMANIZING TEACHER . . .

BUT DON'T STAY IN THE CLASS TOO LONG

I'm an expert in regret. You could say that I have taken graduate courses in the field. It's partly that I've made my full quota of mistakes, so I have plenty for which to feel sorry. But it's also that I have wanted so much to do what is right. Regret is closely related to our desire for excellence. Only the indifferent or the self-satisfied never feel regret.

Regret can be a powerful and effective teacher, but it can also destroy its students. Berthold Auerbach, the nineteenth-century German novelist, said, "Regret is the most stupid feeling one can possibly cherish" (*Little Barefoot,* ch. 17). But on the other side, Henry David Thoreau, the American essayist, said, "To regret is to live afresh" (*Journal,* Nov. 13, 1839). It all depends, you see, on how you deal with the lessons this teacher offers.

Regret is one of our distinguishing human characteristics. You can't feel regret unless you have some measure of reflective intelligence. Regret is possible only for a creature who can stand off at a distance and look at itself, or who can evaluate and analyze its past. Regret requires a certain degree of moral sensitivity. To feel regret you must have some standard of right and wrong—or perhaps, of better and worse. The higher one's level of moral intelligence, the greater one's capacity for regret.

REGRET CAN DESTROY OR REFINE

Left unchecked, regret can destroy a person. Some years ago a minister who had just become pastor of a large church began seeking out families that had been out of touch with the church for an extended period. One evening he called in a home where the wife engaged pleasantly in conversation, but the husband stayed in the next room, obviously choosing to isolate himself. As the minister left the home, the husband followed him to the porch. There he suddenly blurted out, "I killed a kid, you know."

My minister friend soon learned that the man, a city bus driver, had run into a boy, causing the boy's death. It was not the man's fault; he had been completely exonerated. Nevertheless, he could not free himself from *regret*. Day and night he relived the scene, asking himself if he might some way, somehow have avoided the fatal accident. He was captive in a prison house of regret.

46

Some of our most painful regrets are for opportunities lost. As John Greenleaf Whittier said:

> Of all sad words of tongue or pen,
> The saddest are these: "It might have been!"
> (*Maud Miller*, 53)

How many people go under a dark cloud by thinking, even momentarily, of the person they almost married, the investment they almost made, the position they nearly won. But for every person who is filled with regret for an opportunity lost, there is another who regrets a deed done, a word spoken, a relationship consummated. These are the stories of decisions made, of tempers lost, of conversations that cannot be recalled. Here are deeds—sometimes sinful ones, but often only erratic or misguided ones—that have changed the course of a life and have left a person with a crushing burden. "I'd give anything," a man or woman says, "absolutely anything, if I could take back that one day of my life." *Regret*. It can eat at your inward being like the most malevolent cancer, destroying by the inch and the hour. And there is no surgeon's knife, no radium or chemical that can reach it.

Yet, regret can refine and improve character as only a skilled teacher can do. I venture that there are few great saints who have not possessed a high capacity for regret. Effective regret is the growing edge of godliness. But the key word is *effective*!

Saul of Tarsus knew something about regret. His regret was so strong that it surfaced in the midst of a wondrous recital about the resurrection of Christ. As he listed those who had seen the resurrected Christ, he

47

continued, "Last of all . . . he appeared also to me. For I am the least of the apostles, unfit to be called an apostle, because I persecuted the church of God" (1 Cor. 15:8, 9).

This regret could have destroyed the man we know as Paul the apostle. His was such a burden that one could be crushed by it. Instead, he allowed regret to be his teacher. He learned from his mistakes and his sins. He chose neither to minimize his past nor to maximize it, but simply to learn from his errors and, thus, to use them.

LET REGRET LEAD TO REPENTANCE

Every intelligent person has reasons for regret. If the apostle Paul had regrets, why shouldn't you and I? To feel regret is one of our better human characteristics, if out of it comes repentance. Repentance is that act by which we say to God, to ourselves, and perhaps to some concerned human beings that we realize we have done wrong and we're sorry for it—and, more than that, that we will now take a different course. The wrong we've done may be something that has affected primarily ourselves; it may be nothing other than a bad choice or the neglect of an opportunity. Whatever it is, it's important that we face it, confess that it exists, and pledge ourselves to change it.

This is the point of difference between good regret and destructive regret. Good regret leads us to repent and thus to change, and to be rid of the impossible burden. Destructive regret causes us to push the troublesome thought underground, where it begins to eat away at our psyche, or to immerse ourselves in a misery of remorse without actually doing anything to change or to be free.

Those who engage in the Twelve Step program of Alcoholics Anonymous have a prayer that is a perfect guide for dealing with regrets—a prayer, incidentally, that comes from a great modern American theologian, Reinhold Niebuhr. This prayer asks for the courage to change what can be changed, the serenity to live with what cannot be changed, and the wisdom to know the difference between the two.

If the matters for which we feel regret are matters we can remedy, we should do so. If there are mistakes we can rectify, sincere apologies we can offer, hurts we can relieve, we should be about them without delay. By doing so, we can take the sting from regret.

I knew a boy (knew him well!) who once cheated a storekeeper out of two cents. He had a well-trained conscience, and although his family moved from the neighborhood, he couldn't forget the two cents he owed the storekeeper. One day, several years later, he saw the man on a city street and ran to him with the coins. The regret of a minor infraction, long past, now became the deep satisfaction of a debt made right.

A woman realized, as an adult, how much a high school teacher had done for her. She was filled with regret that she had never told the teacher. The regret pursued her and made her unhappy. One day she did a little detective work and located an address for the teacher, so that she could write a letter of gratitude. Regret produced action, and the action brought joy, both to her and to her teacher.

SUPPOSE YOU CAN'T CHANGE THE PAST?

Some things just can't be changed, and immersing ourselves in unrelieved regret will only destroy us. We need the wisdom to recognize those things we cannot change and then, as the prayer says, we must seek the serenity to live with them. A professional football player says that a great quarterback needs to know how to forget. When he throws an interception, he must put it out of his mind and throw another pass as quickly as possible. A television interviewer asked Gregory Peck, the actor, about one of his sons who had taken his own life. Peck answered with obvious emotion, "I probably think of him not only every day, but every hour. But one goes on living."

I think it is the devil's business to keep us so occupied with useless regret that we are unable to do anything about our present opportunities. Regret must never become a dead-end street. It must lead to repentance, sometimes to recompense, and always to action. And if there is no longer anything that can be done, the action is simply to go on with life.

Ralph V. Landis was the resident physician at Lawrence University for over fifty years. Shortly before his death, he recalled for a younger doctor a long-ago regret—something entirely out of his control, but a regret that could easily have destroyed him. He and his wife had two sons. Three days before Christmas, the first son died of scarlet fever—now easily treatable by penicillin—and on Christmas Day the second son died. Landis was so angry he threw the Christmas tree through the living room window.

The bitterest irony came a few years later, when he was stationed at Walter Reed Hospital during World

War II. There he was the first doctor to use the new miracle drug, penicillin. Recalling the experience, he said, "I didn't know whether to laugh or cry when I saw those boys recover as quickly as mine had died."

As the younger physician listened to Dr. Landis's story, he said that he doubted he could have survived such an experience. Landis answered, "I wouldn't have myself if it hadn't been for my wife. She's the one who kept us going and refused to quit. She said we were meant to have a family and we would have one. We raised three more children—our second family. I couldn't have made it without her determination."

In such instances when we cannot directly remedy the errors or omissions or hurts of the past, we have to move on. Such is the insistence of God's grace. It is no wonder that the person who wrote "Amazing Grace" was one who knew something of regret. John Newton went to sea when he was only eleven years old. His life rapidly degenerated into every kind of immorality and crudeness of living. He came to work on slave ships, which must surely have been the vilest of jobs.

Then one day he was converted from his shameful, destructive life. He must have known a continuing torrent of regrets for all the people he had hurt, all the laws he had broken, all the years he had wasted. How could he repair all the harm he had done? As a matter of fact, he couldn't. Should he live, then, in unceasing regret? Some choose, under such circumstances, to do so, using regret as a kind of daily intoxicant that puts them into an emotional stupor. But Newton wisely chose to harness his regret and to put it to use. At thirty-nine years of age, he became a minister of the gospel, and over the years he wrote many hymns. His testimony is sung every Sunday around the world:

> Amazing grace! how sweet the sound,
> That saved a wretch like me!
> I once was lost, but now am found,
> Was blind, but now I see.

Newton put his regret to productive use. He could not repay many of those whom he had hurt in his wasteful years, but he could extend benefit to countless others. And so can we all.

That must have been the attitude of the apostle Paul. He could not restore Stephen to life, nor could he find, again, all those others whom he had persecuted in the time when he was an enemy of the church. But he could pour the energy of his regret into blessing others. There were things he could not change, but he could find serenity by making peace with his regrets and by moving on.

REGRET AND GRACE

Regret is to life what pain is to the body. It is an instructive warning, to help us avoid further, and perhaps worse, anguish and to guide us into more productive living. But regret is not an end in itself. It is intended to lead us along.

I'm sure I never get through a day without experiencing some regret. Some matters are of real significance, while others are of little consequence—my self-rebuke that I didn't see someone in time to wave a greeting or that I was so distracted I didn't give full attention to someone's comments. But whether the regret is large or small, it can help me; it can give a growing edge to my life by giving me an incentive to improve tomorrow.

So I pray that I will never lose my capacity for regret. And I pray just as fervently that I will make my regret a productive factor. Regret is heaven's good gift, probably unique to us human creatures, to help us grow into better, more honorable, more expert human beings. But run amok, regret is fired with the power of hell.

I don't think I would know how to handle regret if I didn't believe in the grace of God—the grace not only to be forgiven, but also to be restored and made better. At the one extreme, I might try to harden myself against regret so that I would never feel its pain. But in that process, I would become less than human. At the other extreme, I might become so burdened with regret that I would come to despise myself.

It must have been at such a juncture that the plain-spoken nineteenth-century evangelist Dwight L. Moody spoke. "God has cast our confessed sins into the depths of the sea," he said, recalling a promise of scripture. Then he added his own homely touch: "And He's even put a 'no fishing' sign over the spot."

That's a great word to remember. With God's grace, we can harness regret. When we have hurt another or have violated the law of God, we can find forgiveness through grace. If we have disappointed ourselves, we can use the regret as a building stone in the erecting of a better life. "I'm not fit to be called an apostle," Paul said, "because I persecuted the church." He had regrets, many of them, very real regrets. But through his regrets, forgiven and sanctified, he became a saint.

5

LOVE IS A BEAUTIFUL TEACHER . . .

BUT THE LESSONS ARE NOT ALWAYS EASY

In one of his most memorable lyrics, Oscar Hammerstein II insisted that you have to be taught to hate; you have to be taught when you're six or seven or eight. But love seems to come naturally. I believe that every baby emerging from the womb desires to love and to be loved. Perhaps it is because the womb itself is a warm and embracing place. Or perhaps love is instinctive to us because we are social creatures; we reach out for love as naturally as we reach for food, simply because we cannot live without it. Or perhaps it is that love is the image of God that is printed on our very being; God is love, and because we are made in God's image, we love, too.

It isn't long, unfortunately, until our love-capacity takes something of a beating. Soon enough we encounter unloving people, and soon enough we are disappointed—rightly or wrongly—by those who love us. But the urge to love remains, and the lessons of love go on continually, for love is one of life's greatest teachers. The lessons are not as simple as they at first appear, and they are surely not always easy. But love is a persistent, strong teacher, and if we give love a measure of attention, we learn in ways that make life very beautiful.

LOVE TEACHES RESPONSIBILITY

There is a little book in the Bible, so short you can read it through in fifteen minutes, that is sometimes described as the greatest love story ever written. At first it is the story of a man and a woman and their two sons. In a time of famine and depression, they move to a foreign country. There the father dies, and the two sons marry local women. Life seems to be moving along pleasantly enough when the two sons also die, leaving three widows—a mother-in-law and her two daughters-in-law.

The mother-in-law's only possibility of survival is by returning to her homeland. Both younger women sincerely pledge their love and offer to go with her, but eventually one of them decides to remain in her homeland. When the mother-in-law, Naomi, insists that the other girl also stay with her own people, the daughter-in-law, Ruth, replies:

> "Do not press me to leave you
>   or to turn back from following
>   you!
> Where you go, I will go;
>   Where you lodge, I will lodge;
> your people shall be my people,

and your God my God.
Where you die, I will die—
there will I be buried.
May the LORD do thus and so to
    me,
    and more as well,
if even death parts me from
    you!"
                    (Ruth 1:16, 17)

Later in the story, Ruth remarries. When her first child is born, the community looks upon it as uniquely Naomi's child because of the deep bond of love between the two women.

Are you a little disappointed in this story? When you heard it was the greatest love story ever told, you thought it might have some of the tenderness of a romance novel, or the excitement of a soap opera segment. You're disappointed that the romantic part of the story involves a young widow and an old woman, and you're especially let down to discover that the lovely words that you've heard sung or recited at weddings—"where you go, I will go; where you lodge, I will lodge"—were spoken by a daughter-in-law to her mother-in-law.

This reminds us that our contemporary idea of love is likely to be very narrow. We think of it primarily in a romantic or a sexual way, and we associate it with feelings of passion and ardor. We don't often think of love in the long pull, the kind of love that shows itself in dogged loyalty.

So what does love teach us? Ruth discovered and demonstrated that love means responsibility. Our first experiences with love don't necessarily prepare us for such a realization. In the earliest years of our lives we usually experience love as recipients; we're cuddled and cared for. We give love in return, but our infant love is an instinctive thing, a simple pouring out of affection.

As a result, most of us are likely to have a rather shallow idea of love. It's something we enjoy, something that makes us feel good, something we show with a hug or a kiss or a kind word. Sometimes love received may even incline us to be selfish; after all, if people are always doting on us, we come to expect such doting. We become people who expect to receive love without understanding love's responsibilities. Some, unfortunately, never get beyond this stage. All of their lives they expect love to flow their way, never thinking that mature love involves responsibility. And responsibility often means sacrifice.

I have nothing against romance; as a matter of fact, I'm a sentimental, romantic person. But romance is measured in ecstatic moments, while love is measured in untiring years.

LOVE IS SOMETIMES A PAINFUL TEACHER

Because love is spelled *responsibility,* it sometimes teaches through pain. When the late Roy L. Smith, pastor and for many years editor of his denomination's national magazine, was not yet eighteen, he received a hurried message at school that his father had been hurt at the mill where he worked. While Roy was running down Main Street in Nickerson, Kansas, a blunt man called out, "No use runnin', kid. He's gone." Smith's father was a skilled mechanic and flour miller, and was highly respected in their little village, so every business in town closed down for his funeral service. The day after the funeral, Roy and his brother went to the mill to gather up their father's belongings—his tools and the work clothes in which he had died.

The first thing Roy saw were his father's shoes, the soles turned up. There was a great hole in each one, stretching from one side of the shoe to the other. On the day Roy's father died, his bare feet were against the concrete floor of the mill. Roy realized that he was himself standing in good shoes that his father had bought for him less than two weeks before. He would have given anything, he said later, if he could only have put good shoes on his father's feet for the last hour of his life (Roy L. Smith, *Tales I Have Told Twice,* 49-53). The experience gave young Smith a lesson in love, but it was a painful lesson.

A song that was popular a few years ago asked in half-playful fashion, "What do you get when you fall in love?"—and after listing some of the disappointments love brings, concluded with the phrase, "I'll never fall in love again." When we first receive love, we think that all of love's lessons are beautiful. But we usually learn before too long that there is a price for love. If you want never to be hurt, don't love anyone and don't let anyone love you. On the other hand, if you refuse to love or to be loved, you will never experience any great heights of joy and fulfillment. Love comes at a price of pain. There is really no way to have love without giving up something of yourself and your freedom, and without making yourself vulnerable. That's why love, beautiful as it is, is a painful teacher.

LOVE PAYS, AND REPAYS

I'm happy to say that love pays, but let me make clear that it doesn't always pay when we expect it to, or in the way we thought it might. In the story of Ruth and Naomi, Ruth gave so much love to Naomi by vowing to stay with her through all the circumstances of life, even to death. She was wise enough to know that Naomi could never really repay her. Naomi had reached an age that would make her Ruth's charge until death; Ruth's promise of "until death" was therefore no idle word. Naomi herself had explained to both her daughters-in-law that there was no future with her.

In its highest expressions, love doesn't really seek payment. It gives because it is right to give, and because the heart and warmth of life demand it. Nevertheless, love *does* pay. There *is* a reward. But it doesn't necessarily come from the one to whom love is extended. Love is the original networking arrangement; it is built into love's very nature. I'm very sure that I didn't love my parents in the measure they loved me, but I have been privileged as a father to repay my parents by the love I've given to my children. In fact, part of the love I have opportunity to share each day is drawn from the deposit that my parents and others gave me long ago.

Naomi didn't repay Ruth directly. She helped her, however, in a crucial juncture, so that Ruth was blessed with a new marriage—to Boaz. It was a beautiful development in Ruth's life. So in the structure of love's mathematics, Ruth gave to Naomi, and Boaz gave to Ruth, and all of them gave to one another.

Love requires repayment. The person who doesn't pass love along finally loses the love that he or she received. Love is a kind of spiritual manna; keep it too long and it will rot. Some of the most unpleasant people on earth are those who have been favored with loving attention but, giving little away, have become the traditional "spoiled brats." And adult spoiled brats are the worst of the breed. Love must be passed along! If there is no one in your circle of life to whom it can be given, go out on the street and distribute it prodigally, wherever you can: in a word here, a smile there, a deed of careless generosity, a letter to someone long forgotten or known only by newspaper reference. Somehow, some way, pass love along. It will spoil if it isn't shared.

LOVE IS SOMETIMES LATE, BUT NEVER TOO LATE

In thirty-eight years as a parish pastor, I presided at hundreds of funeral or memorial services. I cannot estimate how many times I heard words of regret: "I wish I had done more for Mom." "If only I had written more often." And the most frequent: "If only I could have said good-bye."

Some of the expressions of regret were well founded. As a pastor, I knew that some adult children had been neglectful of a parent, and they had good reason to wish now for another chance. A fairly predictable pattern emerged over the years: the son or daughter living far away was usually more shaken by grief and remorse than the one living in the same town with a parent, providing immediate and frequent care.

But even those who have been most attentive, as family or friends, often wish there had been "just one more visit" or "one more chance to say how I really feel." That's a natural reaction; it is itself a product of love, because love wants to express itself and never feels that it has expressed itself fully or adequately.

Frederick M. Hinshaw describes in strong but sensitive fashion an expression of love after death in a poem he calls "Last Act":

> Six weeks after the fainting spell at lunch
> when he broke his hip, the old man died.
> The family had come daily to the bed
> of the half-blind, half-deaf patriarch
> saying, "Do you know me, Pop?"
> and "Are they feeding you? Where do you hurt?"
> and in the night he would cry for help,
> call names of those who came
> and other names as well and plead for death.
>
> As the wife, daughter, and grand-daughter
> filed out after the visit of the nurse . . .
> the weakening, slowing sounds of death,
> (whispered—"Is that what they call the death rattle?")
> the silence . . . they said, "He's gone, now,
> we wish our best to you." Moments later
> the sound of the electric razor started:
> the dutiful son trusting to no-one else
> this final loving task he wanted to do himself.
>   (*The Rotarian*, August, 1981, 9)

That's too late, someone says. The father was dead, so it doesn't matter to him who shaved him for burial. I believe that it *does* matter, and it matters profoundly.

I believe that the act following death almost surely reflects the feelings and conduct before death. It is a continuation of a quality of caring that must have existed for years. But more than that, I believe in the power of love to penetrate those barriers of time, space, and eternity that we usually consider impassable. This is something of what the apostle must have meant when he said in his poem on *agape* love, "For now we see in a mirror, dimly, but then we will see face to face. Now I know only in part; then I will know fully" (1 Cor. 13:12). Love can reach from time into eternity.

Now someone wants to press the issue with me. "Are you trying to say," they ask, "that the father knew his son was shaving him?" Yes, I think that's what I'm trying to say. I'm trying to say that love has a language and a power of communication beyond our comprehension. So it is that love goes on paying those who have loved long after the usual measures of this life are past. I know I can't prove I'm right about this. But come to think of it, no one can prove I'm wrong. I simply believe that because God is love, love can break the otherwise impenetrable barriers of time and space. So while love is sometimes late, it is never too late.

Love is a beautiful teacher. All of us are blessed with some of love's classes, and some of us receive love's lessons in abundance. But to whom much is given, much will be required. Love is sometimes a strict and demanding teacher, because love is strong. But watch love with rapt attention and learn. And as you learn, vow more surely than ever that you will love as others, and as God, have loved you. Go to love's school again tomorrow, because there is no end to the lessons love can teach.

6

ONLY THE TOUGH LEARN FROM SORROW . . .

BUT YOU'RE UP TO IT

Sorrow is one of the primary teachers in the School of Experience. I wish I could spare you Sorrow's lessons, but it isn't possible. Live long enough, and you will experience sorrow. Live even longer, and you will experience even more. So since the class is inevitable, we need to see how we can best learn sorrow's lessons.

Sorrow has to do with the experience of loss, particularly loss in its most dramatic form, bereavement—the death of someone we love. There can be almost the same experience in the loss of a treasured friendship or the breaking of a marriage or a romance, because many of the same emotional elements are involved. Sometimes people say that their divorce was like a bereavement. But other emotions often enter into the ruptures of human relationships, such as anger or a desire to strike back; and, of course, as long as the other person is still alive, one may nurture some hope of reconciliation. I think we can say that the purest form of sorrow is that which comes with bereavement.

DAVID'S EXPERIENCE

Many people think of David, the king and psalmist, as one of their favorite Old Testament characters. The Bible describes him as a man after God's own heart. But David was nevertheless painfully human. He committed adultery with Bathsheba, the wife of one of his army officers. When David learned that she was pregnant, he tried first to deceive her husband into thinking that he was responsible, and failing in that effort, arranged for him to be killed in battle. He thought he had done all of this without being detected, but the prophet Nathan soon came to him with a message of judgment from God. He had broken God's law and had brought dramatic sorrow and hurt to a number of people. The prophet announced that the child who had been conceived in his adulterous relationship would die.

Shortly thereafter the infant fell ill. Though David had been told that the child would die, he nevertheless implored God to spare the boy. His earnestness puts one in awe; he fasted and lay on the ground all through the night. His trusted servants and advisers pleaded with him to forsake his vigil, but he refused.

On the seventh day, the boy died. Who would dare to tell the king? "When the child was still alive," they reasoned, "we spoke to him, and he did not listen to us; how then can we tell him the child is dead?" (2 Sam.

12:18). David noticed that his servants were whispering, and he sensed the reason. "Is the boy dead?" he asked. "Yes, he is dead." David then rose from the ground, bathed, dressed, and went to the house of God to worship; then he came home and ate.

His servants dared to ask for an explanation. Having agonized when his boy was struggling for life, how is it that he could now rise up and return so naturally to the routine of life once he knew the child was dead? David answered:

> "While the child was still alive, I fasted and wept; for I said, 'Who knows? The LORD may be gracious to me, and the child may live.' But now he is dead; why should I fast? Can I bring him back again? I shall go to him, but he will not return to me." (2 Sam. 12:22, 23)

David was a remarkable, deeply spiritual man. He was a sensitive poet, but he was also a pragmatic military and political leader. Very few people in the scriptures, or in secular literature, have expressed themselves with such depths of feeling as David did; yet when he confronted sorrow, he was a pragmatist, dealing with it in the style of a military tactician. Now that this particular battle was lost, he was deploying his emotional forces to another field, so he might win some other battles!

RESIST TRAGEDY AS LONG AS POSSIBLE

David teaches us a major lesson concerning sorrow: Don't enroll in Sorrow's class any sooner than absolutely necessary. So many give in to sorrow prematurely. Some argue, perversely, that it's better to expect the worst, and then if it doesn't happen, you'll feel better! David didn't reason that way. The prophet had told him that his son was going to die. Yet when the child fell ill, David refused to acquiesce to his death. He chose instead to pray, to see if he might get a different result. Whether David's theology was right or wrong, I will not argue; I only know that I admire him for not giving in to despair until there was no other way to go.

Several years ago *Guideposts* magazine told the story of an eighteen-year-old boy who was terribly injured in an automobile accident. He couldn't walk, talk, eat, drink, see—or as far as anyone could tell, think. Whatever life was in him was there only because a machine was breathing for him. The best medical judgment said he could not possibly recover, and that even if he lived, it would be in a vegetative state.

His older brother became obsessed, however, with a commitment to his recovery. He worked with him twelve hours a day, week in and week out. He rejoiced in a pressure of the hand or a tear in the eye—anything that might indicate even the least sign of life and response. Medical experts insisted that the favorable signs the older brother seemed to see were probably imaginary, but he held on. After nearly two years, he was privileged to see his brother restored to nearly full health.

Writing about the experience eleven years later, he says that his brother, who was once thought hopeless, was now well, working, married, and with only a slight residual weakness on his right side. The older brother resents it when people say it was a miracle. "We're ordinary people," he writes, "and we overcame fear and pessimism and poor odds and even cold facts by concentrating totally on hard work and the most natural thing in the world—prayer" (Steven McGraw, "Brother," *Guideposts,* Feb. 1984, 2-7). I am impressed that he did not preregister in the School of Sorrow. Sometimes we give up too soon. We ought to resist tragedy as long as we possibly can.

I feel that way even when the cause proves eventually to be lost. I think of a friend and former parishioner whose husband, a medical doctor, was diagnosed with cancer. The specialists told her it was terminal and she should adjust herself to that fact. She had lived in the medical world most of her adult life, for not only was her husband a doctor but she was herself a nurse. Yet she resented the specialists for taking her hope from her. She wanted, she told me later, to hold on to hope as long as there was anything to hold to, and she didn't want anyone to take it from her. I agree. We shouldn't sign up with sorrow too soon.

LET SORROW BE NEITHER TOO LITTLE NOR TOO LONG

When sorrow does come we should not fear it. Most of us in the western world have been taught to shut up our sorrow and to avoid any release of tears or emotion. We're now slowly coming to recognize that these ancient outlets are both natural and right. There is a time, as the writer of Ecclesiastes said, to *weep.* Tears can clean out some of the emotional backwashes of life. If we hold back tears that ought to be released, we may set grief to eating away at our inner being, where it will do far more harm.

Sorrow, however, can be entertained too long. As Robert Allen has said, "You don't drown by falling in water, you drown by staying there." There is a time to bid farewell to sorrow, or at least to harness it. Long ago a rabbi said, "Who broods excessively over his sorrow will weep for yet another death" (Talmud, *Moed Katan, 27b*). I have seen such instances, and I'm sure you have, too. One thinks of parents who lose a child, and in their unrelieved sorrow, emotionally cut off a remaining sibling. Sometimes when one parent cannot bring sorrow under control, the marriage itself is broken. I remember an older person who brooded unceasingly over the death of a spouse until he slowly cut himself off from his children. Brood excessively, and you will, indeed, "weep for yet another death."

DELIBERATELY TAKE A COURSE OF ACTION

When we experience sorrow, our usual reaction is to hide away with books, music, and memories. A little of this goes a long way! We can too easily wrap ourselves in the kinds of songs and poetry that aggravate our sorrow. King David took the opposite course. His story is marked by a series of action verbs, and the very intensity of those verbs is instructive. He "got up." He had been lying on the ground, prostrate with agony and prayer; but when he knew the baby was dead, he got up off the ground. Prayer had sustained him through the long struggle, but now it was time to rise up and build on his prayers by beginning to live again.

A longtime missionary to India told me of the paralyzing grief he felt after the death of a child. He tried to immerse himself in study and writing, but his grief increased. Then one day, he said, he went into a shed and began to do carpentry work—heavy, tiring work. Ever after he looked back upon that day as the beginning of his emotional recovery. His experience was all the more impressive to me, because he was a deeply spiritual man, the sort of person one might think would find his strength in meditation. "Nothing takes the place of action," he said. "Hard work—*physical work*—is a great friend."

Then the scripture says that David "washed, anointed himself, and changed his clothes" (2 Sam. 12:20*a*). To put it in modern terms, he showered, put on bath powder, then some after-shave lotion. That was wonderful good sense. We can dramatically alter our spiritual and emotional state by what we do with our bodies. Sometimes when we are despairing we can do a world of good for ourselves by simply attending to our physical selves.

David changed his clothes—he had worn the garments of agony and abasement long enough—and "he went into the house of the LORD, and worshiped" (2 Sam. 12:20*b*). Now, above all, he would draw on the strength of the Almighty. Two factors are at work here. After suffering a tragedy we can easily harbor resentment against God. The beleaguered soul asks, "Why should this happen to me?" forgetting that most of the

71

things that happen to us also happen to most of the human race; why should we expect to be exempt? In time of pain, however, we lose that perspective and think the universe itself is against us. In time of sorrow, we need to go to the house of worship to clear away any such feelings of inner anger.

More than that, we need to draw on the strength of the Eternal. Life's deepest sorrows have a kind of spiritual, mystical quality. Though these sorrows happen on this earth, there is nevertheless something unearthly about them. This is especially true of the experience of bereavement; and also, in different measure, of such tragedies as the severing of a cherished relationship or the loss of a job or failure in school. Some elements of our pain are measurable in a laboratory or on a ledger sheet, but other elements are more intangible. They are spiritual, in the truest sense of the word, and we need the strength and mercy of God if we are to cope with them effectively. In the house of God, we set our feet on the bedrock of life. We may think for a time that we are reaching out into empty space, but in time we take hold of the ultimate realities.

Next, when David left the house of worship, he did a very human, ordinary thing, but a profoundly significant one: he went home, asked for food, and ate. How often is the doctor's prescription given: "You must start eating properly." "But I just don't feel like eating," the person in sorrow complains—and some wise soul gives a no-nonsense answer: "Then eat because you need it, whether you feel like it or not." We human beings are spiritual creatures, but we are alsomachinesthatmustbefueledandtended. Omitthat fueling process long enough, or handle it irregularly, and the motor will begin to sputter and die.

David went home and ate! I wonder if perhaps the eating seemed almost a desecration, as if he were being disrespectful of his sorrow. Sorrow sometimes lays such a sense of guilt on its students. But if we don't eat properly, we will stay in sorrow's class so long that we'll fail the course. We need energy to cope with pain and despair, and energy comes from food as well as from prayer and worship. David sat down to eat. I'm not sure he felt like it. Perhaps the food wasn't really appealing. But he ate, because he needed to.

Finally the writer tells us that David consoled his wife Bathsheba. He got out of himself. By its very nature, sorrow can be quite self-centered. Sometimes people in sorrow tell themselves that no one is suffering as they are, shutting themselves into a strangely arrogant private chamber of pain. David was wise enough—and compassionate enough—to know that Bathsheba was in at least as much pain as he was, so he comforted her with the strength he had now received.

In time, Bathsheba conceived again, and they had another son, Solomon. I wonder if either of them said, when the first child died, that they would never have another child? Did they say that no one could ever take his place? If they did, they were right, of course; no human being ever really takes the place of another. But that isn't the point. Life must go on, and we must go with it. We dare not allow ourselves to take permanent residence in the bog of despond.

IT IS WELL, IT IS WELL!

Late in the last century a well-to-do American businessman, Horatio Spafford, sent his wife and four daughters on a trip to Europe. En route, their boat was battered by Atlantic storms. The daughters were lost at sea; the mother cabled home just two words: "Saved alone." I believe it was the following year that Mr. and Mrs. Spafford made the same trip. When the ship was at approximately the same latitude and longitude, Spafford pondered at ship's edge the sorrow of their lives. He wrote, then, words that have since become a source of strength to many:

> When peace, like a river, attendeth my way,
> When sorrows, like sea billows, roll;
> Whatever my lot, thou hast taught me to say,
> It is well, it is well with my soul.

He then went beyond their immediate tragedy, and made theological application to all of life:

> Though Satan should buffet, though trials should come,
> Let this blest assurance control,
> That Christ has regarded my helpless estate,
> And hath shed His own blood for my soul.

Later, two more daughters were born to the Spaffords. Did they take the place of the four who were lost at sea? Of course not; but the Spaffords allowed the strength and grace of God to heal their suffering, and they rose up and went on living.

Each of us must deal with sorrow. It is one of the inevitable courses in the School of Experience. The secret is to learn the lessons well, so our lives are not permanently caught in pain. David, a man of deeply sensitive feelings, could easily have spent the rest of his life with sorrow after suffering the loss of the infant son. He and Bathsheba, already off to such a questionable start in their lives together, could have poured the remainder of life into some pool of bitterness.

Instead, David rose up and started again. He treated sorrow with the respect it so richly deserves, but he didn't build a permanent dwelling there. He moved on—by common sense, by faith, and by God's help—so that he might live another day. He was tough enough to learn from sorrow. So are you and I.

7

SIN CAN BE A
PRODUCTIVE COURSE . . .

BUT DON'T BOTHER TO REGISTER

S in can be productive? Am I recommending sin? No, not at all. But I am a realistic person who knows that, whether we like it or not, people do sin. I know this by personal experience and by observing the lives of others—and few people get to observe more about the lives of others than those who spend years as a parish pastor.

However you define it, whatever dressing you put on it, we human beings have a problem. Job, who knew a great deal about life, said,

> but human beings are born to
> trouble
> just as sparks fly upward. (Job 5:7)

There's some sort of negative impulse loose in our universe. The apostle Paul wanted so much to do what was right, but found that so often he did what was wrong. No wonder he called himself a "wretched man." Mark Twain made the same point with a wry smile when he said, "Man is the only animal that blushes—or needs to."

So it's not a question of whether or not we will sin. The Bible says that all of us do. But will we *learn* from sin? That is the question. I hate to see a person spend hours, days, months in a course and have nothing to show for it. And here's the irony: that's what this teacher would like to happen.

Sin is like no other faculty member in the School of Experience, because sin doesn't really want to instruct us, but to destroy us. That's why I wouldn't take a single course from sin if I could help it; but since I seem to get into Sin's classroom from time to time, I've decided I must make the most of it. I'd like to frustrate this teacher by learning from the course—even graduating, if that is possible!

SIN IS A PATIENT TEACHER

I wonder how many hundreds of times I have quoted Frank Satterlee, and how many more times I have altered my conduct because of what he said. Mr. Satterlee was my Sunday school teacher when I was about ten years old. I expect his academic advantages were few, but he worked hard preparing his lessons. Most of all he impressed us boys when he would lay down his quarterly and tell us of his years of carousing and rebellion, and then of how God came into his life. Not only did he learn from his sins, he tried very hard (and with much success) to keep others from repeating the courses that had given him so much pain.

I wonder if Adam and Eve tried to teach Cain and Abel about sin. Did they explain that life can be an Eden if we refrain from sin, and did they say how easily life's glory can be tainted, then demolished? If they did, Abel learned from their instruction and Cain did not.

Cain was a farmer and Abel a shepherd. In time they brought their offerings to God, and while both offerings represented a personal investment, Cain's was rejected by God while Abel's was accepted. Cain became very angry, so that "his countenance fell" (Gen. 4:5). God, with the divine humility that marks all of the biblical story, reasoned with Cain. "Why are you angry, and why such a long face? If you do what is right, you will be accepted. But if you do not do what is right, *sin is lurking at the door*" (Gen. 4:6, 7 paraphrase). God went on to explain that sin desired to get Cain, but that he must master it.

Unfortunately, Cain didn't choose to rule over sin; he let sin rule him. He nurtured the anger that was in his heart as if it were a delicate flower, until the anger grew into a plan, and the plan into an act. One day Cain urged his brother to go to a field with him, and there in the field, away from any restraining voice or hand, he killed him. But murder was only the concluding scene in this drama—sin was at work long before the act itself.

Country folks used to describe some people as being so kind, they'd even say a good word for the devil. I'm not anxious to say a good word for sin, but I know that to understand sin we need to see how patiently it goes about its work. Sin doesn't have to get its results today or tomorrow or anytime this year. Believe me, most sins do not come upon us as orphans. If someone commits murder or extortion or adultery, you can be sure the act has a long ancestry.

This is what Jesus meant when he said that if we hate our brother, we are murderers, and when he warned that the man who looks at a woman with lust in his heart is guilty of adultery. Sin is a creature that grows. It begins small and relatively harmless, usually as a thought. Generally we can justify the thought: "I have a right to be resentful." Or, "What harm will that do? A little thing like that?"

We laugh when Professor Harold Hill in the musical *Music Man* warns that the boy who buckles his knickers below the knees is "on the road to degradation," but despite the laughter there is a truth here. There's no harm, directly, in most of life's little misdemeanors, but they grow. An ancient rabbi said, "Sin begins as a spider's web and becomes a ship's rope." You and I add those strands that change the spider's web into a rope; but because we add just one strand at a time, and because each one is usually so small, we don't realize what we're constructing. Sometimes, on the other hand, the growth seems to happen almost of its own accord. It is as if we planted a seed in the soil of the soul by some small act of sin and, without our seeming to attend it or care for it, it develops into a full-grown tree. Sometimes, verily, a forest!

One way or another, sin grows, and the teacher Sin is patient to await its fruition. That's a lesson we ought to learn from Sin, and the earlier we learn it, the better off we'll be. Cain didn't begin with a bloody knife in hand. He began with a thought: resentment that his brother seemed favored above him. Actually, the problem must have begun even earlier, in whatever quality of life caused his offering to be unacceptable (unbelief, according to the book of Hebrews [11:4]). Perhaps the problem began when Cain and Abel were quite young. Did Cain, as the older brother, resent the attention his parents paid to Abel, the infant? Such feelings are natural enough. "What harm can they do?" we wonder. But these feelings must be faced intelligently. Otherwise they will grow, until the strands of the spider's web become a rope that binds and, eventually, strangles.

SIN IS A MASTER OF EXCUSES

I hear Cain arguing with himself after receiving God's chiding. He thinks God has treated him unfairly. Perhaps he questions God's judgment. I remember times when, in my own mind, I argued with teachers who had corrected my papers: "What makes them think they know so much?" It's very difficult to say, flat out, "I'm wrong." I can usually find justification for my misdoings. Sometimes I even bathe them with virtue! Someone has said that our greatest security against sin is our being shocked by it. The shock response is hard to come by in our day. We are fed such a constant "diet of shock" in the media that we're not likely to be shocked by anything so subtle as passing thoughts of evil. Besides, our culture excuses most conduct, including even the most reprehensible, by shifting the guilt to others.

81

Criminologists say that the incarcerated almost never accept responsibility for their deeds; instead, they point to persons and influences that have made them what they are. But that shouldn't surprise us, because most of us have the same problem with our "lesser" sins. Even in marriage and in cherished friendships, we find it hard to say, "I was wrong. The fault is mine."

The book of Leviticus, in a section dealing with rituals of forgiveness, has a lengthy series of sins that persons commit "inadvertently," or as another translation puts it, "unintentionally." We usually think of sin as an intentional act or a deliberate word or thought. Is it possible to sin "unintentionally"? Is it fair to call an unintentional act a sin?

I believe the scriptures are trying to show us that though our intentions may not be wrong, we may still do harm to others, so that the effect on our "victim" is the same as if we had intended to do harm. I think of instances in my life when I've said the wrong thing to someone because I didn't know the other person's point of sensitivity. I meant no harm, yet I did harm. It was not a sin in the nature of my intention, but it caused the same measure of pain.

When the Hebrew law required persons to make a repentant sacrifice for such "inadvertencies," it forced them to examine themselves and to face and confess the harm they had caused. Such a response is calculated to make a person more sensitive in the future.

If we are to learn from sin, we must be willing to face ourselves with unremitting honesty. We must be done with those clever euphemisms that make our conduct

less distasteful, and we must stop looking for scape-
goats—society, parents, circumstances—to share
our guilt. While it is true that most of our shortcomings are aided and abetted by persons and circumstances, any attention to these matters diverts us from
taking our lives in hand. Sin is a master of excuses.
It rarely faces itself, and almost never admits itself
at fault. This quality of sin has become more sophisticated in our time, when we have learned so many
synonyms that are more palatable than "I have
sinned." We explain, "I'm a Type A personality, you
know"; or perhaps, "I've never been very good in
that sort of situation"; or even, "In some ways, I'm
probably a little socially maladjusted." We've
learned a lot since Cain!

YOU CAN WIN!

The most important lesson to learn from sin—and
the lesson sin tries never to speak—is this: we can win!
We are not helpless in the face of sin. God has invested
in us the capacity to win in this eternal and apparently
unceasing struggle.

This was the word of hope that Cain received. "Sin
is lurking at the door; its desire is for you, but *you must
master it*" (Gen. 4:7 author emphasis). It is a hard,
realistic word. Sin is pictured as a beast ready to spring
on us, a mythological creature that *desires* us. There's
nothing soft or casual about that! We're involved in a
real fight with an utterly malevolent enemy. But we can
win!

I knew a man years ago who was a vigorously earnest Christian. When people praised his intensity, he would explain that he had been a full-fledged sinner. Now that he was a Christian, he was resolved to serve God with the same energy.

Life is on the side of such logic. The same power with which we do wrong is available for us to do right. Dr. E. Stanley Jones used to say that when we are converted, it is not that we receive new abilities and capacities, but that our old capacities and tendencies are transformed and thus redirected. The gossip doesn't become a silent person, but one who uses the tongue for good rather than evil. The person who was formerly a lecher does not cease to reach out to others, but does so now with caring love rather than with lust. We can win over sin.

The first step is to seek the forgiving grace of God in Christ. This puts sin in its right perspective, as an act that concerns God and therefore as one in which I can expect God's help. Having enlisted God's help, I have everything going for me. (Still a lot against me, mind you, but much more going for me!) The New Testament writer, wanting to encourage believers who felt themselves undone by sin, reminded them that "the one who is in you is greater than the one who is in the world" 1 John 4:4). We rarely realize the extent of our potential under God.

But if I am to learn from this teacher who dogs my steps through all my days, and who wishes more to fail me than to teach me, I must constantly remind myself that even the smallest sin is a peril, because sin grows, and the teacher Sin is patient to await its fruition. And

SIN CAN BE A PRODUCTIVE COURSE

I must never excuse my sins, but confronting them, I must learn. And above all, I must never forget that, with God's help, I can win. God didn't intend for us to be losers. The power and personality with which we sin are the very gifts with which we can serve God most nobly. *That* should show the teacher!

8

SUCCESS IS A FUN COURSE . . .

UNFORTUNATELY, YOU MAY NOT LEARN MUCH FROM IT

If students in the School of Experience could always choose their teachers, there is no question who the favorite faculty member would be. All of us, or nearly all, would make Success our major professor. We would specialize in its courses—the more advanced and sophisticated, the better.

But there is a problem with this curriculum. Though Success is a popular teacher, it's not usually an effective one. Or perhaps, as with many teachers, the fault lies in the students. We probably don't understand how to learn from Success.

SUCCESS IS HARD TO DEFINE

One reason we don't learn much from success is because we don't necessarily recognize success when

we see it. When Hamilton College celebrated its cen-
tennial, one of its most famous alumni, Alexander
Woolcott, was asked to give a major address. Horace
Fenton, Jr., remembers that Woolcott opened his speech
this way: "I send my greetings today to all my fellow
alumni of Hamilton College, scattered all over the
world. Some of you are successes, and some of you are
failures—only God knows which are which!" That's
why it's hard to learn from success. We don't always
know it when we see it.

✳ Sometimes we think ourselves successful when
we've won some competition, when in truth we may
have been mediocre or less, and we survived only
because the competition was even worse. Sometimes
we think ourselves successful simply because we have
such poor standards that we accept shoddiness as an
achievement.

On the other hand, sometimes we fix our eyes so
firmly on a particular goal that we overlook some very
real achievements of another kind. I'm told that Beatrix
Potter never found great satisfaction in her Peter Rabbit
stories, which have blessed so many millions, because
her pride was in her work as a natural scientist. Clement
Moore was a professor of Oriental and Greek literature
at Columbia University for twenty-nine years. He produced a Hebrew dictionary and some books of fine
poetry. But one Christmas season he wrote a little poem
for his children, which within a year or two was bringing laughter to children everywhere—to this very day,
in fact, over 150 years later. It begins like this:

> 'Twas the night before Christmas,
> And all through the house,

Not a creature was stirring,
Not even a mouse.

The poem always embarrassed Professor Moore. He knew it was not great poetry. It certainly wasn't in the style of the Greek and Oriental literature he explained to his students each week. But for children and parents around the world, he is a success, for the measure of magic he has brought into our lives.

You may have heard of "The Peter Principle"—the theory that every employee in a hierarchy tends to rise to his or her level of incompetence. People achieve in some phase of work, but instead of recognizing this success and developing it, they decide they ought to be something else—generally something that represents more money and more prestige. So people go on to a position in which they may do poorly and in which they find less satisfaction, because they didn't appreciate success when they had it. Of course, it's hard to learn from success if we aren't sure of the definition.

A LESSON IN GRATITUDE

There was a man long ago who got a good definition of success early in his career. He was a king, but he was wise enough to know that this was, in itself, not necessarily a measure of success. After all, there are good kings and bad kings. As a matter of fact, it is especially hard to be a successful king. While on the one hand you can do things your own way, in so

89

doing you lose the built-in correctives that govern most of our lives.

Early in his career this king, Solomon, had a dream. In it, God said to him, "Ask what I shall give you." That's quite an offer, when the One making it has every resource at easy disposal! Solomon answered, first, by thanking God for the blessings his father David had enjoyed and for making him king in his father's succession. Then he pleaded, "Give your servant therefore an understanding mind to govern your people, able to discern between good and evil; for who can govern this your great people?" (1 Kings 3:9).

Solomon had already enjoyed several successes. If there had been political commentators in his day, they would have spoken positively of his first hundred days in office. He had been tested by several enemies, and he had handled the problems promptly and well. But what is impressive is that he apparently learned from his success.

Solomon teaches us a huge lesson: to have a sense of gratitude. Since no one is really self-made, this lesson ought to come easily to those who succeed; they have more reason than others to recognize the degree of their debt of gratitude. Yet so many successful people forget those who have contributed to their achievement. Solomon realized that his father, David, had taken a beaten, divided people, and had forged them into a strong, proud nation. Now it was his privilege to build on what his father had done.

Of course, that was only the beginning of what Solomon owed to others. He might well have considered the prophet Nathan, who had gotten his father back on track when he lost his moral integrity. If Nathan hadn't challenged David's conduct, there might not have been a kingdom for Solomon. And how much did Solomon owe to his mother, Bathsheba? Or to those generals, advisers, and loyal staff people who stayed by his father when the kingdom was being torn from him by Absalom? Solomon was a success already, but he was standing on the shoulders of a multitude to whom he was in debt. The same is true for anyone who succeeds in any field. Success ought to teach us that, but because of the nature of success, many students— perhaps even a majority—miss this lesson.

Several years ago I offered the invocation for commencement exercises at a large state university. I remember one unprogrammed event above everything else. At a strategic point, the president of the university invited the graduating students to applaud their parents and spouses, in appreciation for helping them reach this wonderful day. It was a moving moment.

The president might also have invited the students to applaud their professors and librarians, the authors of their textbooks and of journal articles, the people who preceded them in research, and the citizens whose taxes had paid most of the cost of their education. It would be a long list—and a gloomy one for any egotist who might have thought he or she was self-made. Above all, the president could have invited the students to bow in gratitude to God, the Source of life, breath, health, and talent—including the vast mines of talent that most of us never begin adequately to explore.

A LESSON IN REMEMBERING

Along with gratitude, success should give us a good memory. It doesn't always do so, but it should! People who succeed so often forget what made them succeed, until their success slips from them. I've known executives who got to their high post by being daring and imaginative; but in the executive office they become too reserved, sacrificing their best talent. Most of us have known salespeople who built a loyal following by their attentiveness to every detail of their customers' needs; but with success, some of these same people become so hurried they all but brush off the very people who got them where they are. It happens to entertainers, too. They build a following by loving people, but with success they begin to feel superior to their crowds. Slowly the people slip away from them. They forget the secret of their success.

God often gets the same treatment. I'm sorry to say that it was so in the case of Solomon. In his early success, Solomon leaned on God; he knew the source of his strength. But as time went by, he seemed to forget God. Success itself may have been partly responsible; as people told him how wonderful he was and how much they admired his wisdom, Solomon must have begun to think the wisdom was his own doing. Wealth got to him, too, causing him to live with shameful abundance and with little heart for those who had less. As Solomon's life drew to its close, he was a pathetic creature, worshiping numbers of pagan gods. He had become cruel and unfair—this man who once had prayed for an understanding heart! He forgot the God who made him a success and the qualities of character that were once the secret of his achievements.

Success ought to give us a good memory: for God, for people, for the abilities that enabled us to achieve. But ironically, success often causes a lapse in memory—a strategic, even fatal, lapse.

A LESSON IN EXCELLENCE

For fifty years, my friend Margaret was the private secretary for a series of top-flight executives. In her retirement she frequently contributed her talents to our church office when we needed extra help. Working with successful business people had given her a high regard for excellence. She insisted that everything must be perfect. One day I asked her to retype a letter, because of a mistake in my dictation. I had dreaded asking her to do the letter again, since she was contributing her time as a volunteer, but to my surprise she was elated when I made my request. "I've been afraid you were letting some errors go through, just to protect my feelings. I'm so glad you want it done right! Nothing should leave our office unless it is perfect."

Baltasar Gracian includes in his lessons from life, "I learned that mediocrity within yourself is unacceptable." Success teaches us to expect the best from ourselves. The most successful people need no other quality control; they're harder on themselves than any critic. And if there is any word they despise, it is the word *mediocrity.*

Malcolm Muggeridge titled his short biography of Mother Teresa *Something Beautiful for God.* My idealistic soul says that each of us should do our work with that motto in mind—particularly when what we do is done for Christ and the church. The song we sing, the report we give, the class we teach must be excellent—as truly excellent as we can make it—because it is done for God. It was such a passion for quality that made J. S. Bach identify each composition—including those that were written on secular themes—as "for the glory of God alone." Bach's vision of success was one of excellence, and his standard for excellence was that his work should be acceptable to the praise of God.

SUCCESS HAS BUILT-IN HAZARDS, BUT HUMBLE STUDENTS WILL PREVAIL

Success ought to breed success, but it doesn't always work that way. In fact, success has no greater danger than itself. When Roy Tarpley entered the National Basketball Association, it was assumed that Dallas could build a team around him. Experts say he would have made the American "dream team" for the Barcelona Olympics if he had fulfilled his obvious talent. Instead, when he should have been at the top of his game, he was not even in the NBA. "My problem," Tarpley said, "was with success. Every time I was successful, I had to go out and party" (*The Plain Dealer,* March 24, 1993).

The problem with success *is* success. This reminds us again of the importance of godly character. Success has within it the seed of failure and even of self-destruction. The more success a person achieves—including the most honorable and praiseworthy success—the more one needs the correction of the Holy Spirit.

I'm very sure God wants us to succeed. It is better that we become saints than corrupters, better that we use God's generous gifts rather than letting them lie idle or perverting them to unworthy purposes. God, the ultimate Source of success, would like for us to succeed and to learn from each success. But that calls for sensitive students, who never feel that they are above correction and reproof. In other words, the greatest lesson success can teach us is the humility that makes us keep on learning.

9

DEFEAT IS A REQUIRED COURSE . . .

NOT AN ELECTIVE

It was half time in a National Basketball Association game, and the interviewer was hard at work on Isiah Thomas, a Detroit Pistons player and one of the all-time stars of professional basketball. "It's commonly thought," the interviewer said, "that you're a sore loser. Is that a fair statement?"

Isiah pondered only momentarily, then grinned as he said, "Am I a sore loser? Yes, losing never sits well with me." Thomas went on to say that if a player gets comfortable with losing, he's on his way out.

A professional athlete has to develop great toughness regarding defeat. Even the best professional basketball teams rarely win two-thirds of their games in a season, and good teams struggle to get safely over the .500 mark. That means that a player goes home from nearly half his games stung with defeat.

The odds are about the same for life in general. Defeat is a required course. No one escapes it. Some, unfortunately, seem to stay in last place most of their lives, but even those whose lives seem to be a stadium decked with pennants have had more defeats than anyone can imagine. In many instances, the major difference between the pennant winners and the last-place folks lies in the way they have handled defeat.

Defeat comes in all shapes and sizes. It can be as inconsequential as losing a Ping-Pong match with a sibling, or as crucial as a malignancy. Some defeats come because we have entered a situation that was clearly a win/lose scenario, like a political campaign or bidding for a contract, but others come in experiences that we hadn't thought of as life-contests, like marriage or raising a family. Defeats are sometimes public matters, known throughout the community or within one's profession, while sometimes they are so private that not even a spouse or closest friend knows. Defeats take on importance out of proportion to their true size; most of us can remember some elementary school defeat that still lingers in the memory, and that still stings.

But don't let defeat terrify you. It's far too commonplace to be given that power. Rather, see defeat as a primary teacher—an unavoidable one, and an unwelcome one, but one that can give a depth, a height, and a breadth to our lives that cannot be received from any other teacher.

DEFEAT IS A COURSE, NOT A CURRICULUM

Once there was a man named Joshua, who was marked for winning from his birth. I say that on the

98

basis of his name, which in Hebrew means "savior." It's quite astonishing that his parents gave him such a name, because he was born into a slave family and a slave nation—a nation that had known nothing but slavery for generations. Somehow his parents had high hopes for him even before his birth. Such expectations go a long way toward a person's positive self-image, and eventually toward one's achievements.

When Joshua was still a relatively young man, he became a first assistant to Moses, the epochal leader of the Jewish people. When twelve persons were selected to make a reconnaissance trip into the land that the Israelites planned to invade, Joshua was one of the twelve. Ten of the committee came back with a negative report, but Joshua chose, along with Caleb, to make a minority report. He believed in winning, and he was confident that his nation was capable of winning, no matter what the majority felt.

As it turned out, forty years went by before Joshua's convictions were put to the test, and when they were, he was the commanding officer. On his first campaign, he won a stunning victory, the battle of Jericho. The odds were dramatically against Israel; they were not an army, but an unknown, untried body of people only a generation removed from slavery, and they were marching upon one of the most impregnable fortress cities of their time. But they won, and won big.

Then they marched on to the city of Ai. This looked easy, compared to Jericho. Instead, however, they suffered a humiliating defeat. Joshua didn't handle it well. "O Lord," he cried, "what can I say, now that Israel has turned their backs to their enemies!" (Josh. 7:8). Joshua was so done in that he accused God of poor judgment in bringing the nation this far only to see them defeated. He warned God, with the insight we human beings sometimes offer to the Almighty, that people everywhere would soon be mocking the divine name as a result of this defeat.

Many of us can empathize with Joshua's reactions to his defeat. It's easy to see any loss, even a minor one, as the end of everything. Most of us can remember some occasion when we interpreted a particular rejection as the end of our world. I once asked a very successful sales executive if he had ever felt like quitting. "Every day," he said. "Every time I call on a prospect and am turned down. Even after years of success, I have to argue with every defeat that comes my way. I have to take it by the scruff of the neck and tell it I'm bigger than it is. And sometimes I think I'm lying when I say it!"

God didn't let Joshua wallow in defeat. "Get up!" God said. "Why are you lying on your face?" Then God told Joshua to search out the reason for his defeat. That is, God told Joshua to let defeat be his *teacher.* Nothing would be accomplished by lying on the ground crying, "We've lost, we've lost!" Defeat has value only as we find out *why* we've lost. Defeat is a course, not a comprehensive curriculum.

Joshua learned they had been defeated because they had sinned. He searched out their sin, found it in a man named Achan, and dealt with it. Then he was ready to move on, and he did so with a victory at the place where shortly before he had been a loser.

WE CAN LEARN FROM DEFEAT WITHOUT BEING DEVASTATED BY IT

I don't know of any really fine person who hasn't studied well in the course of defeat. Sometimes our defeats come in the field of our eventual achievements and sometimes in some other areas of life. It doesn't matter too much where we study defeat as long as we learn from it and come to apply its lessons across the broader spectrum of life. The lessons we learn will vary according to our personalities and the nature of our needs. A key lesson for business success may have little to do with establishing an effective family life. Perhaps that's why we take so many courses from defeat; the courses don't easily cross register in the School of Experience.

A key rule, then, is to learn, not be destroyed. Probably no one in American history is more revered than Abraham Lincoln, and probably no one in public life knew more about defeat. Early in life, he lost in love. His career was a struggle against odds, with many failures. He went through a series of almost unremitting political defeats before being elected president, and for that matter, he suffered constant public deriding during his presidency. His private life was equally torn. In a letter to his friend John Stuart, Lincoln said: "I am now the most miserable man living. If what I feel were equally distributed to the whole human family, there would not be one cheerful face on the earth. Whether I shall ever be better, I cannot tell; I awfully forebode I shall not" (*The Collected Works of Abraham Lincoln*, vol. I, 229).

Yet clearly enough, Lincoln learned from his defeats. When he stood at the edge of his greatest victory, he spoke with the wisdom and compassion that can only be learned through defeat: "With malice toward none, with charity toward all. . . ." Assassination prevented Mr. Lincoln's ever having the chance to implement his convictions, but he was settled in his mind as to the course he would follow. I don't believe that he would have possessed such compassionate insight if he hadn't himself suffered so many losses. He had a soul for those who had lost because he had learned the pain of defeat. If he had not learned from defeat, he would have struck out against the conquered with bitter revenge. His education in defeat made him great.

I had a professor in seminary who was a favorite with nearly all the students. He was a fine scholar and an effective lecturer; but most of all, he was a compassionate, sympathetic man. He had time for his students and a heart for their problems. Gradually some of us came to know his story. We learned that he had been victimized by an unscrupulous colleague in graduate school, so that his best research was taken over by another man. He had a physical ailment that caused him almost constant pain. But he developed a strong devotional life, which enabled him to gain from his defeats a mellowness of spirit and empathy for others.

Perhaps no major defeat of a personal nature is more prevalent today than divorce. Whatever the reasons in any individual case, the parties involved almost always feel defeated. They look back on the dreams with which they entered marriage and agonize over the shattering of those dreams. Even those who are blind enough to lay all the blame on their partner are still likely to feel defeated deep inside. In some instances, they maintain the bravado pose because they don't want others to know how deep are their feelings of defeat.

But the lessons learned from the defeat of divorce differ widely. Some seem not to learn much; either they come out of the relationship with an abiding hatred of the opposite sex, or they enter into another and perhaps several equally disastrous unions. Others examine themselves and their defeat, and in time become better human beings and better equipped in human relationships.

I had a brother-in-law who was an electrician. As a boy, I watched with fascination as he repaired items that ran on that mysterious power called electricity. One day he made a careless mistake, and when he plugged in the item he got a jolting shock. He grinned and said, "Now I know *that* wasn't the right solution." I thought about him years later when a member of my parish was showing me through the research unit of his manufacturing firm. One engineer's desk had a framed message: "Babe Ruth struck out 1,330 times." A research engineer has to remember that there are more strikeouts than home runs. He has to be ready to say, after another failed effort, "I must be closer to the solution, because I've just eliminated another incorrect possibility." The secret is to learn from the error, not to be devastated by it.

DEFEAT HELPS KEEP LIFE IN PERSPECTIVE

If we win all the time—or if we think we're winning when in fact we're not, for sometimes we fool ourselves—the elements of life get out of proportion. As a matter of fact, we need an occasional defeat to help us remember that God is God. Many people in public life—especially entertainers, athletes, and politicians—come to believe their own press releases and to think they're above the rules of ordinary human beings. Wealth does the same thing to many people.

What happens in these more prominent positions happens also at every other level of life. We see it on the playground, at the community club, in the classroom, and, saddest of all, in the family circle. It's painful to see someone broken by defeat, but sometimes it is the most important experience a person will ever have.

It can be hard to know God if we're so enchanted with our own successes that we become unduly fascinated with ourselves. Even as good a man as Job learned that. After his devastating losses, he was exposed to the glory of God: "I had heard of you by the hearing of the ear, but now my eye sees you" (Job 42:5). I know a woman who is both a gracious hostess and an outstanding teacher. Several years ago she was stricken with multiple sclerosis. Now she must walk with a cane, and she lives with the prospect of further limitations. Recently a few of us at a dinner party asked her how it was going. She startled us by saying, "MS has been wonderful! I would never want to be the kind of woman I was before it afflicted me." To tell you the truth, I thought she was a fine person before this illness, but

DEFEAT IS A REQUIRED COURSE

I'm sure she knows what she is saying. God and life and values have come into new perspective for her as a result of her continuing physical "defeat." She is already turning her "defeat" into a special kind of victory.

Defeat's effect on our relationship to other people is especially significant in keeping life in perspective. If we never know what it is to lose, we have little compassion for the human race. Too many victories can make one unkind and insensitive to the feelings, limitations, and problems of others. Someone says, after seeing another human being fail, "I can't imagine committing such a sin." Can't you, really? Are you made from a better grade of clay? Are you not part of the human race? If we can stand in judgment on another person's failure without feeling a sharp and intimate sense of empathy, God have mercy on us! If we have been so long without a defeat, or if we have forgotten the feeling of failure, or if we are unable to relate the quality of our own weakness to that of another person's shortcomings, our soul will become a mean and narrow thing.

WE DON'T HAVE TO TAKE THE SAME
COURSE AGAIN AND AGAIN

While defeat is a great teacher, it is limited, as are all teachers, by the willingness and the aptitude of its students. A teacher is only as effective as the students allow her or him to be. Defeat is almost without a peer in the dramatic, incisive way it makes its points, yet some of us will not learn from it.

Some simply refuse to apply the lessons. They complain that they can't see why such things should happen to them; they wonder how life can be so unfair. Others seem to insist on taking the same lessons again and again. People have come to me as their pastor, saying in despair, "Well, here I am again. It's the same old story." In such instances I've sometimes wanted to ask, "Why are you taking this course again? Did God ask you to repeat it? If not, why insist on covering the same material you've already belabored for so long?" But I've never said it. I've repeated too many courses of my own in the Classroom of Defeat, so I know better than to raise questions about others. Nevertheless, let's remind ourselves that defeat has no desire to see its pupils a second time. Defeat prefers that we take the course once, and move on.

I have said that I don't know of any really fine person who has not studied well in the course of defeat. On the other hand, I've known many who seem to have learned nothing from their defeats. They come out of their experiences harsh, bitter, and meanspirited. Their occasions of defeat have not beautified or refined them. Instead, they have become resentful of life.

Life has been good to me. As a boy I had many dreams, many of which were out of proportion to the world in which I was growing up, yet most of them have come true—in greater measure, in fact, than I could have imagined in my limited view of life. I have enjoyed far more than my share of kindness from others, and to my continuing astonishment and gratitude, such kindness continues to flow.

But as I look back on my story, I realize that my greatest blessings have come by way of my defeats. Growing up in poverty—a defeat thrust upon me by circumstances beyond my control—gave me an understanding of people that I could not have gotten from textbooks. I loved sports and wanted, like many young people, to be an athlete. But I had such a poor sense of coordination that I not only couldn't make school athletic teams, but also I was even the last to be chosen on playground pick-up games. When you're a teenager, that's a big defeat. But it helped me understand those whose intellectual coordination was as poor as my physical variety. I began dreaming of college when I was eleven years old—a foolish dream in my neighborhood—and I didn't get there until I was nearly twenty-five. But the waiting made me a more discerning student and a more passionate lifelong learner. A failed marriage has given me more heart for the pains and failures of others, and a greater reluctance to pass judgment.

Defeat has seemed at times to be an unconscionably harsh teacher; but in review, I realize it is only because I have been so slow to learn. Defeat would have been satisfied to treat me more kindly if I hadn't insisted on advanced and elective courses! I am grateful that eventually I've been willing to learn. In at least some phases of my life, I have gotten to the point where I seem to have graduated. And believe me, I'm holding tight to my diploma!

In the School of Experience, there are only a few required courses, and defeat is one of them. It is not so bad to lose a battle at Ai, as Joshua did, if only we learn from the defeat. Then, farther down the road, we can understand what the apostle meant when he said that we are "more than conquerors" through Christ our Lord (Rom. 8:37). Somewhat scarred perhaps, but bright with learning, we will be conquerors, too.

10

You Can Learn from Your Enemies . . .

It Will Frustrate Them to No End

S
he hasn't an enemy in the world," someone says of an especially winsome person. It's a lovely compliment, but of course it isn't true. All of us have enemies— not necessarily because we want it to be so. The psalmist complained that when he was for peace, others were for war (Ps. 120:7). Try as we will, we will not please some people. Sometimes, in fact, people dislike us because of our trying; something about goodwill irritates them, perhaps because they are so given to ill will. In some instances people dislike us because we're on the opposite side of some question, and sometimes because they don't understand us. But sometimes people dislike us for good reason, at least from their point of view. They may even be right! It's quite possible they would cease being our enemies if we would change something of our conduct, or our

attitude toward them, or if we would make right some earlier wrong, whether real or imaginary.

Enemies are a fact of life. If you will read through the entire book of Psalms within a short enough period to get the feel of the book, you will be surprised to see how many of the psalms deal with the issue of life's adversaries. The Bible is never so Pollyannaish as to pretend that evil doesn't exist, or that kindly feelings are lurking everywhere, waiting to embrace us. It recognizes that there is a waywardness in our world and that, as a result, we have to deal with such unpleasant matters as enemies—large and small, real and imagined, human and mythical.

Because enemies exist, we should make up our mind to learn from them. After all, they're part of life—part, that is, of the School of Experience. Sometimes, in fact, they're a vigorous and vocal part. We need to learn how to deal with them, and we need to learn from their example.

WHY IS THIS PERSON AN ENEMY?

The first question that must be answered is why is this person an enemy? If the enmity is on our part, we need to know why we feel as we do, so we can do something about it. Is it a petty thing, something really not worth such a strong feeling as enmity? After all, enmity involves a tremendous investment of emotional energy, so it shouldn't be wasted! Or has this person really done us wrong—and if so, are we allowing the wrong to control our life long after we should have dealt with it? Could we bring an end to the enmity by some

110

judicious, gracious contact? To do so would benefit us at least as much as it would benefit the enemy, because when we get rid of an enemy, everyone is a winner.

It's ironic, but sometimes we dislike and avoid someone because his or her defects mirror our own. Someone has said that there is no sadder moment in the life of a parent than that day when they see their own failings reborn in their children. Often the matters that most irritate us in another person, even to the point of making him or her *persona non grata,* are our own shortcomings drawn large and visible in the other person's life. If we can become objective enough to recognize this in a particular instance, we could be "rid" of an enemy and at the same time reform ourselves.

Sometimes people become our enemies because they are part of a cause or a movement with which we disagree, perhaps even to the point of despising the movement's supporters. It's difficult to separate people from causes. If the cause is our enemy, individuals easily become personifications of the cause; and human as we are, we find emotional relief in having a person on whom to concentrate our anger instead of something so nebulous as a point of view. If you listen to radio talk shows, you hear people say almost unbelievably cruel things about public officials. I'm sure they don't really hate these political leaders as violently as their language suggests; in most cases, they don't even know them beyond a television sound bite. But hating a point of view, they hate the person who, for them, represents this point of view. As good as it is to be concerned about causes and issues, it is dangerous and destructive to allow a cause to make someone our enemy.

LOVE YOUR ENEMIES OUT OF EXISTENCE

Edwin Markham, the American poet and educator from earlier in this century, was passionately committed to several great causes. A man of such strong convictions couldn't help but make enemies. But Markham knew how to deal with his enemies. In his poem "Outwitted," he wrote:

> He drew a circle that shut me out—
> Heretic, rebel, a thing to flout.
> But Love and I had the wit to win:
> We drew a circle that took him in!

Markham could well have been reflecting Jesus' counsel: "Love your enemies and pray for those who persecute you" (Matt. 5:44). Greek scholars say that the word that is translated by our sometimes inaccurate word *love* would be best translated, if it were a noun, as "unconquerable benevolence." That's a powerful way to deal with an enemy! In truth, it's the only way to get rid of one. You see, the death of an enemy doesn't destroy the enemy's power. If we don't allow "unconquerable benevolence" to take over, our hatred for an enemy will continue to eat away at our souls long after an enemy dies—and when that happens, the enemy, ironically, is still winning! Only as we learn to love will we be rid of an enemy.

A significant part of that achievement comes through the second portion of Jesus' command—that we pray for our enemies. It is nearly impossible to pray for someone yet go on hating them. I can't promise that the enemy, in turn, will change his or her outlook toward you, but the odds are substantially better than if you, too, are hateful. Love will work its miracle in your heart, even if the object of your prayers seems untouched.

DON'T LET YOUR ENEMIES CHANGE YOU FOR THE WORSE

Whatever you do, don't let those who have wronged you remake you in their image. When three young men were brought to trial in a West Memphis, Arkansas court for killing three eight-year-olds, the father of one of the victims suddenly rushed at the young men screaming, "I'll chase you all the way to hell!" I understand the father's fierce anger, but there is something almost prophetic about his words. If we allow our hatred for those who have wronged us to go unchecked, it will eventually destroy us. We will follow our bitterness "all the way to hell."

Friedrich Nietzsche warned, "When you fight a monster, beware lest you become a monster." A police officer tells me that in his profession there is a constant danger of becoming brutalized by the work, until one becomes like the people he or she apprehends. Sometimes parents do this in a way that may seem amusing to an observer. Exasperated with a small child's conduct, a mother or father will sometimes get into a shouting match in which it's hard to tell which is the six-year-old and which is the parent!

Booker T. Washington was born a slave but came in time to be the most influential African American leader and educator in the United States. His achievements were made against fierce odds, including the treatment he received from racists and those who resented his accomplishments. He vowed, however, that he would never allow anyone to make him "stoop so low" as to hate them. He insisted on returning good will for evil; he didn't take on the image of his enemies.

The late Harry Emerson Fosdick applied this insight at the level of international politics at the height of World War II. In a sermon at Riverside Church in New York City, which he titled "Worshiping the Gods of a Beaten Enemy," Fosdick warned that America might easily take on the character of the nations she was fighting. He drew upon a story from the Hebrew scriptures about a time when Judah defeated the Edomites and Judah's king, Amaziah, brought back the idols of the Edomites and "set them up as his gods, and worshiped them" (2 Chron. 25:14). Dr. Fosdick said that all history teaches at least one lesson about war: inevitably it tends to lead the victor to take on the character of the vanquished.

SOME ENEMIES ARE WORTH HAVING

Earlier I mentioned the prevalence of enemies in the book of Psalms. Some scholars feel that in many instances the psalmists are thinking not so much of individuals or even of nations as they are of what might be called "mythical enemies." By that phrase they mean those very real but intangible matters such as malice, immorality, brutality, and injustice. These were the "enemies" that inhabited the individuals and nations that the ancient writers opposed.

These are enemies worth having! I think of an elderly minister who would often say, "Keep a protest in your soul!" We dare not acquiesce to evil; there must always be in us a sense of horror at the injustices that exist in the world and against the brutalities and immoralities that seem sometimes to go unchecked and unopposed. We must remember that certain kinds of conduct are our enemies, and we must take action against them. Martin Luther King, Jr., insisted that the person who passively accepts evil is as much a party to it as those who help to perpetrate it, and that accepting evil without protest is really cooperating with it.

Very little of worth has been accomplished in our world except as someone has dared to recognize an enemy and enter battle against it. God works through the enlightened, disturbed conscience of individuals. We need desperately to have vast numbers of persons who know that pornography, prejudice, poverty, and facile indifference are our enemies, and who will untiringly oppose them. God have mercy on any person who can go idly through life without feeling anger about the forces of evil that exist in our world.

This is something of what the apostle Paul had in mind when he wrote: "For our struggle is not against enemies of blood and flesh, but against the rulers, against the authorities, against the cosmic powers of this present darkness, against the spiritual forces of evil in the heavenly places" (Eph. 6:12). There are enemies in our world; we ought to know it, to face up to it, and to do everything in our power to oppose that which is evil.

USE INNER ENEMIES FOR YOUR PURPOSES

Not all intangible enemies are at the cosmic level, by any means. Each of us struggles daily with enemies we cannot see but which are painfully real. I speak of such inner opponents as fear, resentment, anxiety, a sense of personal worthlessness—the list could go on and on. These enemies harm us in a measure that no person could ever imagine—though sometimes persons are instruments of these inner enemies.

As you will readily see, several of the teachers in the School of Experience would also fit into this category, such as regret or loneliness. In every instance, the rule is the same: treat these enemies with respect, but know also how to laugh at them—or perhaps I should say, know how to laugh at yourself in relationship to them. I find that it often helps if I will admit that my fears are ridiculous, or if I will allow myself to be amused by the way I'm allowing resentment to take residence. Some of the saints have said that the devil is afraid of our laughter; the same can be said for many of the feelings that distress and undo us.

Like enemies in time of war, these mythical creatures should be taken captive and made to serve our purposes. I remember a roughhewn but highly original woman from my childhood. Someone said to her rather playfully, "You're surely a smooth character, Molly." Quick as could be she answered, "I ought to be. Life has been sandpapering me for a long time." She had learned to use the powers that might easily have oppressed her. She acknowledged their peril, but she was satisfied that Christ had invested in her the ability to fight back. Fight she did, and she laughed as she did so!

116

CHOOSE YOUR ENEMIES WELL

In an imperfect world, there will always be enemies. When it comes to people, be sure that you are not the initiator of hostilities, and be sure as well that you are doing everything in your power to correct the problem. Having done all you can, don't blame yourself unduly if ill feelings remain. Sometimes people and circumstances need time; and one person, no matter how possessed of goodwill, cannot solve a relationship problem single-handedly.

In the realm of issues and causes, be glad you're capable of taking on enemies. Maltbie Babcock challenged an earlier generation with his hymn, "Be strong! We are not here to play, to drift." The message is as true as ever, though the hymn rarely appears in contemporary collections. We have the wondrous opportunity to ally ourselves with great causes. They will stretch our hearts and, at times, crush us with disappointment, but they are God's call. Be glad you can be an enemy of prejudice, hunger, war, and crude living. Put on your armor day after day and march out against all such enemies.

As for those inner enemies—fear, worry, regret: don't be afraid of them. By the grace of God, you're bigger than they are. Take them captive for your own personal development. Use them to make you a wiser, stronger, more adequate human being.

Enemies are a fact of life, so choose your enemies well. A person has only a certain amount of emotional energy to spend on conflict. Too many people spend all their energy in petty matters, resenting people, imagining hurts, tilting self-centered windmills. As a result, they have nothing left with which to engage themselves in battle for causes that matter or stand alongside someone who is being beaten by life. Be a careful steward of your capacity to fight evil. God has work for us to do, and we want to do it well.

11

PEOPLE ARE TUITION-FREE COURSES . . .

TAKE EVERY POSSIBLE CLASS

Tuition generally runs high in the School of Experience. You can tell that by the names of some of the faculty—Pain, Sorrow, Regret, Defeat. This is also why the institution's popular name, the School of Hard Knocks, is thought by many to be its official name.

But there's one bargain course in the school. The teacher is usually pleasant. How pleasant? He or she pays the tuition! You can't ask for a better deal, can you? One wonders why this class isn't more enthusiastically attended. I suppose it's because it calls for a high degree of humility, and for many of us humility is itself a painful price.

This teacher is *People,* people who have already paid the price of experience or of accumulated knowledge. Why reinvent the wheel? If someone else has already taken a particular course, it's far less expensive to learn from them than to insist on paying full tuition.

BE WILLING TO LEARN FROM AN UNLIKELY TEACHER

I could illustrate the benefits of this teacher in any number of stories from the scriptures, because the Bible is full of mentoring relationships. But I've chosen an incident from the life of Moses because it illustrates that we can learn much from even the most unlikely teacher.

If anyone might have been justified in depending on his own counsel, it would have been Moses. He is still looked upon as the first great deliverer, for bringing the nation of Israel out of slavery in Egypt. He has a special place in the history of law because of his association with the Ten Commandments. I read the account of his life in a standard encyclopedia to see how secular history treats him. The rather lengthy summary of his life and accomplishments faithfully covered the highlights in his legendary career—of which there are many. But the encyclopedia left out what I consider to be one of his finest hours. In some ways, this incident is basic to many of the rest of his achievements. It isn't dramatic, but some of our most significant experiences come in quiet settings.

This experience occurred not long after the Israelites had escaped from Egypt. They were settling into a somewhat structured existence, but it was a slow process. When you have thousands of people living together, you inevitably have disputes. And when the people are living as nomads, the possibility of such

120

disputes is exponentially increased. Still worse, these were people who had lived in slavery all of their lives; they had no tradition of self-government, not even a memory from their parents or grandparents. They were ill-equipped to survive under even the best of circumstances, and believe me, their wilderness life was not the best of circumstances!

Moses had to deal with these disputes, and it was an almost endless job. You can imagine: someone complains that his neighbor in the next tent is disturbing the peace, playing his harp late at night. Another insists that a fellow is letting his flock feed in the first man's territory. All day long, hour after hour, Moses listened to arguments and points of view. Some of them were truly important issues, but most were not. Yet all of them took time and energy. And because there were so many to be heard, people had to stand in line for hours, waiting their turn. It was a miserable system, exhausting for Moses and frustrating for the people.

Then Moses' father-in-law, Jethro, came to visit. He watched this day-long scene, then quietly and respectfully gave Moses a suggestion. "You're wearing out yourself and the people," he said. "Why not set up a series of judges. Let them deal with the cases and refer only the most difficult to you. That way everyone will get quick justice and you'll have time to do other things." Jethro was suggesting a system of appeals courts. It was a wonderfully sensible idea.

The big question, however, was this: Would Moses be willing to learn from someone else? Moses could so easily have huffed and puffed and said, "Dear father-in-law, you've probably forgotten that I am a graduate of the finest university in Egypt. Furthermore, I challenged the Pharaoh in a series of public debates, and I won. And if you don't mind my asking, have you ever led a group of slaves out of bondage, through the waters of the sea, and organized them into a nation? Specifically, in case you've missed my point: if I ever want your advice, I'll ask for it." That's the way Moses might have responded. That's the way many of us respond when we get a chance for a tuition-free course in the School of Experience—the school of someone else's experience, that is.

But the scripture reports that "Moses listened to his father-in-law and did all that he had said" (Exod. 18:24). He was willing to learn from another person. He was willing to learn from a person with less education than himself. He was even willing to learn from an in-law!

When the book of Deuteronomy sums up Moses' person and career, it puts him in a class all by himself: "Never since has there arisen a prophet in Israel like Moses, whom the LORD knew face to face" (Deut. 34:10). He was someone who often got his directions straight from the Almighty. But he didn't allow his level of spirituality to blind him to the ability God had invested in others. He had the humility and the good sense to know that God might speak to him through some other human being—including a human being who, it might appear, knew less than he did. As a result, his nation was given a more efficient judicial system, and Moses saved his energy for the more significant and more demanding elements of leadership.

Every person has his or her own little store of wisdom and experience. When I was eighteen years old, I spent a wonderful summer traveling with a male quartet. We sang in a different city nearly every day, and we were almost always entertained in private homes. This was before the time of dishwashing machines, so I often slipped into the kitchen after meals to volunteer to help with the dishes. As the summer went along, I discovered that I was learning a great deal during these dishwashing excursions. I concluded that there is a vast store of insight and assorted information in our world, and that everyone has at least a small share.

Of course, as you already know, some people are easier to learn from than others. In fact, some people have a style that makes it almost impossible to give them an earnest hearing. They affect a person in such a way that you can feel your hackles rising the moment they begin to speak. I remember such a person in a church where I was pastor. His manner put me off. I had to learn, with studied effort, to close my eyes to those personality factors that got in the way of learning from him. The attractiveness of a teacher's personality (or the lack thereof!) may have little to do with the quality of the lesson.

Age is often another barrier that makes it difficult for us to learn from certain individuals. We must remember, however, that there are no age requirements in the School of Experience, and there is much to be learned from teachers of every age. Older adults, for example, may prove to be extremely helpful—as long as they are wise enough to avoid such phrases as, "When I was your age . . ." Those who have been on the road of life for many years generally know something of its detours, its traffic jams, its perilous curves. And while the world changes dramatically, it's surprising how little the basic issues change. The stuff of life remains pretty much the same from one generation to another, except for a change of clothing.

We can learn, too, from the other end of life's spectrum. The other day a young father shared with pride a moment from the day before when his three-year-old daughter had said suddenly, "You're the best daddy in the whole world!" I wonder why we adults don't show such spontaneous affection. How much happier our world would be if we were more childlike in our warmth. "Yes," someone warns, "but think how often we would be hurt." Perhaps so, but I think it is worth the risk. Life needs more unspoiled expressions of caring, because such expressions bless both the giver and the receiver.

I'm old enough that I'm sometimes cautious about the "younger generation," as I'm sure they are about my generation, but I wrestle with that feeling because I know I can learn from them. As we grow older, we tend to be overly cautious—perhaps because of the defeats we have suffered. That's why young business people sometimes open whole new fields, and why young scientists sometimes make discoveries that have been missed by experts in the field. In airports I sometimes listen in on youthful conversations. Now and again I learn something I didn't know—about music, computers, entertainment, fashion, and a multitude of other things. I also learn much from my children, who are now at early stages in their careers. Their youthfulness provides a perspective that I have lost.

Of course, we must be discerning in what we learn from others, carefully separating the wheat from the chaff. A person can be a great poet and a poor economist, a powerful leader and a dismal parent, an able student and a fumbling friend. We need to know when to accept counsel from others and when to say "No thanks." Although common sense and trial and error are perhaps the most common guides in this regard, when in doubt we can always seek the advice of others whose expertise in a certain field is proven. In any event, we are being helped by the experience of another.

LEARN FROM THOSE WHO HAVE FAILED AS WELL AS THOSE WHO HAVE SUCCEEDED

Of course, it's fun to learn from people who have succeeded. Regardless of our chosen career, we all benefit from listening to those who have achieved in our field. But we also learn from those who have failed. In my own profession of many years, the parish ministry, I have noticed that some who are quick to offer advice are those whose own track records are dismal. In such cases I have profited not from what the person has told me, but from what I know of the person's mistakes and from the gap between the person's intentions and achievements. We learn from poor examples as well as from good ones.

Go to a library some idle afternoon and look over a few issues of a national news magazine. In no time at all you will have a list of persons in politics, business, or sports who seemed at one time to have everything going their way but now are forgotten or even discredited. We can learn much from people who have failed unnecessarily.

It's as important to know how life can go wrong as to see its possibilities for going right. Some evangelists from my youth told some pretty hair-raising tales about people who had gone on to destruction, but I learned from them. Those stories, even though drawn with bold and indiscriminate strokes, helped me avoid some of life's pitfalls.

I remember a high school classmate who had all the natural gifts of a star athlete. Not only did we believe he was guaranteed to be our starring halfback, but we also calculated that he would lead Central High to her best season in years. In time, however, he dropped out without making any impact. I learned from him that no talent is sufficient to make up for an absence of self-discipline and perseverance. In the intervening years, that lesson has been underlined by numbers of persons in my personal and professional experience. We all can learn from people who have failed unnecessarily.

A LONG LEGACY OF TEACHERS

We can learn not only from people who cross our paths in person, but also from those we meet through books and history. C. S. Lewis said that one of the major factors that influenced him to renounce atheism and accept Christianity was the knowledge that some of the historical personalities whom he most admired were believers. If we human beings would be humble enough and wise enough to learn from history and biography, every generation would be an improvement on the previous one. Somehow, we are reluctant to do so. Don Marquis, author of the charming *archy and mehitabel* series, said:

> a [person] who is so dull
> that he can learn only by personal experience
> is too dull to learn
> anything important by experience.
> (Don Marquis, *archy and mehitabel*)

That could well be the epitaph of our human race.

It is now a truism that those who will not learn from history are destined to repeat it. Philosophers question whether history is circular or linear; that is, does it repeat itself? In some measure, it does indeed repeat itself, because we seem content to learn the same lessons again and again. In some instances we repeat the lesson because we deny or will not face the facts that are unpleasant. Hardly a half century after the Holocaust, one out of every five Americans say they believe it never happened. Why? In some instances it is because of ethnic prejudice; but also, in many cases, it is because people find the facts so upsetting that they deny their existence.

My professional life has been enriched and blessed by my reading of biographies of others in my field. I think especially of Phillips Brooks and Samuel Shoemaker, great Episcopal clergy of the nineteenth and twentieth centuries respectively. But I have also been influenced by fictional characters, especially in my youth. As a boy I was introduced to books by Horatio

Alger, Jr. The plot line was always the same; it probably could be summed up in the title of one of his novels: *Strive and Succeed*. The Alger books convinced me that anything was within my reach if only I would work hard and live with integrity. It wasn't a bad lesson!

TEACHERS, TEACHERS EVERYWHERE!

When I look back on my life, it seems I have been surrounded by teachers. What a faculty I've enjoyed! Some, like my parents and close friends, taught me for years; others within my profession or in a classroom have touched my life for shorter periods. And some, like people I've met on buses, planes, and trains have sometimes left significant lessons within an hour's time. I think of a mother in her late thirties, traveling from Tennessee to Cleveland, Ohio, for crucial, highly specialized surgery. Her strong, straightforward faith still works in my soul to this day. She knew I was a minister; she didn't know that I was her pupil.

We human beings are wonderfully bound together by our common membership in the human race and by our mutual hungers and longings. Because this is so, we can be of so much help to one another if we're humble enough and perceptive enough to share and to learn. A wise, unknown poet testified to this fact:

> It is good for me that I was humbled,
> so that I might learn your statutes.
> (Ps. 119:71)

Most of us learn better after we are humbled. This is especially true in the classroom of People, because we won't learn from someone else until we can acknowledge that he or she knows something we don't. Sometimes that's a difficult concession, especially after we have achieved some measure of success. Perhaps that's why some of us stop growing; having gained position, we find it harder to confess how little we really know.

Moses had a relationship with God that was very nearly unique. He communicated with the Divine as directly as anyone who has ever lived. When his father-in-law came to him with advice, Moses could so easily have answered, "If I need help, I'll get it straight from God." But Moses was wise enough to realize that when his father-in-law gave him good insight, it *was* the voice of God. God was speaking to him through the experience and the wisdom of another human being.

So it is that God comes, often, to our aid. "Here's a bargain," God says, "a chance to learn something without paying for it. Another person has already paid the tuition in the School of Experience, and now I'll speak to you through her. Listen carefully. This is one of my favorite ways of helping you—through other people."

12

YOU CAN LEARN FROM DEATH . . .

HURRY, BEFORE IT'S TOO LATE!

Larry King is a tough-minded pragmatist. He has managed, through a long career in a highly competitive field, to be not only a survivor, but also a winner. Some say that through his interview program on CNN and his column in *USA Today,* he is capable of electing a president. When the interviewer on "60 Minutes" asked King about some possible threat to his career, he answered, "The only thing I worry about is dying" (CBS, Sept. 18, 1992).

With that sentence, Larry King reduced matters to their irreducible elements. Everyone is going to die. When Claude Thompson, a beloved theology professor at Asbury and Candler seminaries, learned that he had an inoperable malignancy, he commented, "The most certain thing about life is death. At the last census the death rate was 100 percent. The ratio of deaths per capita is one to one—one death to one person."

Since that's the case, you may wonder why I include Death in my list of great teachers. Since we expect to die only once, whatever we might learn from the experience seems superfluous; after all, we won't get a chance to put it to further use!

The issue, of course, is not the experience of dying but *death*. It's true that we die only once, and for that reason, we shouldn't approach it as novices. We ought to learn about death so that when our once-in-a-lifetime occasion comes, we will handle it well.

Actually, all of us are exposed to the death process almost daily. Nature offers unending lessons in the flower that withers in its container and the leaf dropping from a tree. Each day the newspaper carries a page or more of obituaries and death notices. We drive past funeral homes. And as we grow a bit older, we lose friends and acquaintances and family members to death with rather alarming frequency.

Nevertheless, we don't know death the way our ancestors did. A typical nineteenth-century home had one room with a door wide enough for a casket to pass through, because the "viewing" and often the funeral service took place at home. Until well into this century, nearly everyone died at home. Ours is the first age in which a majority of people die in institutions, such as hospitals and nursing homes—although the new emphasis on hospice care may change that. On the whole, we are not as close to the experience of death as were our ancestors. And while most of us are probably glad that we don't have to encounter death as intimately, it may also be true that we are poorer because of this isolation. One should not be morbid about death, thinking about it unduly, but neither should one be a fool. All of us are going to die, so we would do well to see what Death would teach us, before it's too late.

There are three ways we can "study" Death. One, of course, is to come close to death, where we see it as a very real, immediate possibility. I've had that experience only once, and it passed very quickly. Yet even in the matter of a moment or two, my mind covered a great deal of territory. Another way to study Death is to see others die. Military chaplains have that kind of experience, and so do nurses; and less frequently, medical doctors and clergy. But we can also study Death by allowing ourselves to contemplate the setting of death.

John Donne, the great seventeenth-century poet and divine, chose for a time to sleep in a coffin in order to discipline his thinking about life and death. That doesn't appeal to my taste, but there is another way to contemplate the setting of death. J. Barrie Shepherd said that one of the things he missed most about Sunday mornings in the United States, as compared with his native Scotland, was the graveyard. In his little village, there was a cemetery around the church—just as there is in some of our rural communities today—and every Sunday morning he and the other worshipers would walk through the maze of tombstones to enter the house of worship. There was something about that walk, Shepherd said, that made the words of life, sung and spoken later in the church, seem more meaningful and more relevant to the realities of the rest of the week.

I was always grateful, during my years as a parish pastor, that my work gave me rather frequent opportunity to visit cemeteries. I think I always left the cemetery with a more wholesome attitude toward life and its purposes. The cemetery reminded me that I have an appointment that cannot be canceled—we all do. We may be able to postpone it, but eventually we will fill it. Being reminded of that appointment brings a more substantial quality into all the rest of our activities.

DEATH IS PART OF LIFE

There was a man long ago—tradition says it was Moses—who recorded his feelings about life and death. He had a wonderful knack for setting his own life and experience into the larger context of his nation and his ancestors, and also into the context of God's range of time. He began this way:

> Lord, you have been our
> dwelling place
> in all generations.
> (Ps. 90:1)

It's good for us to see that there's more to life than just our own times and our own concerns. The writer realized that God had been watching over his ancestors for unnumbered generations. That realization gave him a basis for evaluating his own limited years.

Over the past thirty years I have preached a number of times at a camp meeting that is related to a family reunion. The cemetery in back of the taberna-

cle may be the most popular spot on the grounds. Every
afternoon people wander through it, sometimes to stop
by the graves of loved ones but often simply to draw
upon its quiet strength. Every year someone takes the
younger children through the cemetery to point out the
burial places of key ancestors, to remind them of their
family heritage. They learn that God has been their
dwelling place for at least half a dozen generations!

More than that, this cemetery is the favorite court-
ing ground. Tradition says that a marriage proposal
that takes place in the family cemetery guarantees a
successful marriage. Over the years family members
have come from nearly every part of the country in
order to present the question formally in this setting.
Obviously it is a friendly place, not a foreboding one.
At the place of death, young couples celebrate the
prospect of the future, and little children learn of
their roots. They learn that death is part of life,
inevitable but not dreadful, to be prepared for but to
be neither feared nor solicited.

That writer of long ago captured the mood of this
realization when he continued:

> For a thousand years in your
> sight
> are like yesterday when it is
> past,
> or like a watch in the night.
> (Ps. 90:4)

I suppose that could make a person feel insignificant.
On the other hand, it is wonderfully reassuring to think
that the One who is so much beyond us still cares for

us, and that while the ages roll on, God's mercy endures.

NUMBER YOUR DAYS!

The writer goes on to say that the normal course of a person's life is "threescore and ten" (seventy years) and that our years are lived under the judgment of God. Then he prays the prayer of someone who has wisely pondered the prospect of dying:

> So teach us to number our days
> that we may get a heart of wisdom.
> (Ps. 90:12 RSV)

Wise, indeed! He realizes that his days are, for sure, numbered, so he wants to get a proper sense of the numbering.

I'm not suggesting that each of us has an appointed time, and that the length of our days has been divinely set. I don't really think so. You and I can determine at least something about how long we will live by the way we treat our bodies and by the hazards to which we expose ourselves, but we know that we're not going to live in these bodies, as now constituted, forever. There will be a terminal point sometime. The writer prayed that he would be a good accountant of his precious inventory of time so that he would recognize the limits of his resources—and therefore, more likely, use them well.

Shortly before his crucifixion, Jesus said that he had completed the work God had given him to do (John 17:4). Likewise, the apostle Paul confided to his younger associate, Timothy, that he had finished his course, had kept the faith, and now was ready to move on (2 Tim. 4:7, 8).

Rather early one recent winter morning, I received a long-distance call from a woman whose pastor I had been more than thirty years before. "Mother is about to die," she said, "and she wants to say good-bye." Her mother hardly sounded as if she were dying when she came on the line. "Free at last," she said, "thank God almighty, I'm free at last!" She had lived exuberantly and generously for nearly ninety years, and now she was dying the same way. She felt her work was done, and now she was ready to go. A day or two later, she did so.

One doesn't come to such an assured home-going unless there has been some accounting in earlier years. That's what the psalmist must have had in mind. He wanted to number his days now, so that he could be wise in using this most ephemeral of resources, time. Suppose you or I knew that we had one year, two years, five years to live: how, then, would we use those years? What friendships would we nurture? Where would we travel? What books would we read? How much time would we give to prayer? How frequently and with what intensity would we go to church? "Lord, teach us to number our days, that we may get a heart of wisdom."

DEATH TEACHES YOU HOW TO RELATE TO PEOPLE

The most important issue in this life, next to being rightly related to God, is to have a right relationship

137

with our fellow human beings. As a matter of fact, these two right relationships go hand in hand. Jesse Jackson once told a Democratic National Convention about his visit with the late Senator Hubert Humphrey just three days before Mr. Humphrey died. Humphrey had just called Richard Nixon, and many people wondered why. They had been longtime opponents, both politically and philosophically. Sometimes the differences had been bitter. When Jackson asked Senator Humphrey why he had made such a call, Humphrey answered, "Jesse, from this vantage point, with the sun setting in my life, all of the speeches, the political conventions, the crowds and the great fights are behind me now. At a time like this you are forced to deal with your irreducible essence, forced to grapple with that which is really important to you. And what I have concluded about life—when all is said and done, we must forgive each other, and redeem each other, and move on."

How wonderfully wise! Senator Humphrey had the good fortune to be able to clear his accounts before dying—and he had the wisdom to do so! He had an illness with a fairly sure terminal point. With that in mind, he got down to some foundational matters: "We must forgive each other, and redeem each other, and move on." Sometimes, after someone has died, we wish we had cleared a misunderstanding with them. Just as surely, some people die wishing there was still time to take care of such business. If it's good enough for death, isn't it even better for life?

I will always remember a late afternoon visit with Rhoda Messner. She had been a faithful member of our church for so many years. Now she was dying, and she knew it. Her doctor had told her how many months she had to live, and the predicted limit was near. Our visit that day was pure joy. She explained that the last three months had been marvelous. She had arranged for visits with family members and friends, had written special letters, had made important phone calls. She was ready to go!

Our first instinct is to say, "What a way to go!" True, and since that is so, why not seek, as much as is possible, to live that way all of the time? That's one of the wonderful lessons we can learn from death.

YOU DON'T HAVE TO BE A NOVICE AT DYING

In the motion picture *The Proud and the Profane,* an army nurse is assigned to Iwo Jima. Her husband had been killed there during World War II. After much inner struggle, she musters the courage to go to the cemetery where he is buried. The person who cares for the cemetery is himself a shell-shocked veteran. He was with her husband when he was killed in action, so the wife addresses a number of questions to him.

Finally she asks, "How did he die?" The soldier answers, "Like an amateur. They teach you how to hurl a grenade and how to fire a mortar, but nobody teaches you how to die. There are no professionals in dying because nobody comes back to tell you how."

It's a stirring statement, but John and Charles Wesley would argue with it. They taught people how to die. Think of the language of this hymn by Charles Wesley:

Servant of God, well done!
Thy glorious warfare's past;
The battle's fought, the race is won,
And thou art crowned at last.

There is both poise and victory in such a view of death.

But someone might point out that those words were written by someone who was very much alive. What about someone who was really, surely dying? Not long after Charles Wesley was born anew spiritually, he went to a prison to preach and minister to several men who were sentenced to die. They were converted. About a week later, Wesley went with them to their place of execution. "They were all cheerful," Wesley wrote, "full of comfort, peace, and triumph." They were sure of their destination after death. Wesley said, "I never saw such calm triumph, such incredible indifference to dying." He concluded, "That hour under the gallows was the most blessed hour of my life" (Charles Wesley, *Journal*, July 19, 1738).

John Fletcher was an Anglican rector who some say was as great a saint as ever lived. In the last hours of his life, a man came to see him. Afterward he said, with awe, "I went to see a man that had one foot in the grave. I saw a man that had one foot in heaven" (George Lawton, *Shropshire Saint*, 95).

When you hear of those who die with such confidence and inner peace, you realize that it is possible to learn how to die. It isn't usually a quick course, though it's interesting to see that those convicts with whom Charles Wesley ministered covered the material in barely a week! The secret, I'm sure, is to know *whose* you are, and *where* you are going. If you are confident that you belong to the very Lord of life, death is merely a servant of the occasion. And if you are headed to a home with Christ and those who have preceded you in faith, death is a very *blessed servant.*

We ought to live this life with all the vigor and excitement we can manage—and we ought to live it with the knowledge that someday it will, definitely, end. Because we know it will end, we should prepare for a grand and thankful exit, through Christ our Lord.

VALEDICTORY:
THE SUM OF IT ALL

L ife is an exciting adventure. I believe in heaven, but I believe just as earnestly in celebrating the journey to that destination.

There was a time when popular American religion thought of this world as "a vale of tears." Godly folks sang that heaven was their home, and they found this life a struggle to endure. Life's best merit, it sometimes seemed, was simply to prove one's ability to last it out. The mood of contemporary popular religion is often just the opposite. People don't talk as much about heaven, but instead about the prosperity and good times their faith brings them on this earth. There is a kind of popular theology that suggests that if one is a good Christian, life will always be a swimmingly beautiful affair.

I think both views tend to be one-sided. Without a doubt, this world has its struggles; to deny this is simply to turn off our critical judgment. It's also clear, however, that this life is to be enjoyed. The scriptures—perhaps more clearly in the Old Testament, but just as surely in several of Paul's epistles—tell us that God will make us "more than conquerors," even while we are in conflict with the darkness of certain passing days.

In a sense, that's what this book is about. This life on earth is, on the one hand, a school of preparation for the world to come; but it is also a life to be lived here and now, valuable for its present moment as well as its eternal connections. It is a life that contains struggle; but it is one in which we can learn to win—one, in fact, in which it is God's will for us to win.

The first-century apostle told his people that they should not be "surprised at the fiery ordeal" that was testing them, "as though something strange were happening" (1 Pet. 4:12). Such rigors of faith were to be expected. After all, we live in a world that has gone wrong, a world that is out of tune with God's perfect purposes. So it is that we pray, "Thy will be done, on earth as it is in heaven." It is a world in which the will of God will not be done except as we pray and labor to make it so. We ought not be surprised, therefore, that there are battles to be faced.

In many respects the battles are the same, regardless of a person's faith. Believers and unbelievers alike have to face bereavement, and in most cases, some occasions of sickness. Both believers and unbelievers are victims of the economic cycles of inflation or depression, and both have to contend with the international tragedy of war. The Christian and the person working next to him or her suffer in the same way if their firm relocates or eliminates their department. Being a Christian doesn't move us out of this world, nor does it make us exempt from the various cycles of life.

Being a Christian, however, *does* give us a greater capacity for dealing with those cycles. "The world is full of suffering," Helen Keller once said. But then she continued. "It is also full of the overcoming of it." Everybody has reason to speak Keller's first sentence. A Christian ought to be extraordinarily equipped to speak the second.

Christians sometimes escape some of the problems that come to the lives of others, simply because their life-style keeps them out of trouble. It is now pretty well established that godly living pays benefits in physical and mental health. But eventually all of us have to cope with problems large and small. And that's when we discover some of the real grandeur of our faith.

That's why we enter each day in the School of Experience with a smile. We won't pretend that we like all the teachers equally, or that we anticipate a class in suffering with the same enthusiasm as a class in love. But we know we will benefit from every class. We're utterly sure that in everything God is working with us for our good. For that reason, we expect to make every class count. After all, we're not in this alone.

Suggestions for Leading a Study of
IF EXPERIENCE IS SUCH A GOOD TEACHER, WHY DO I KEEP REPEATING THE COURSE?

JOHN D. SCHROEDER

This book is designed to introduce the reader to some of life's teachers in the School of Experience. To assist you in facilitating a discussion group, this study guide was created to help make this experience beneficial for both you and the members of your group. Here are some thoughts on how you can help your group:

1. Distribute the book to participants before your first meeting and request that they come having read the introduction and Chapter One. You may want to limit the size of your group to increase participation.
2. Begin your sessions on time. Your participants will appreciate your promptness. You may want to begin your first session with introductions and a brief get-acquainted time. Start each session by reading aloud the snapshot summary of the chapter for the day.
3. Select discussion questions and activities in advance.

Note that the first question is a general question designed to get discussion going. Feel free to change the order of the listed questions and to create your own questions. Allow a set amount of time for the questions and activities.

4. Remind your participants that all questions are valid as part of the learning process. Encourage their participation in discussion by saying that there are no "wrong" answers and that all input will be appreciated. Invite them to share their thoughts, personal stories, and ideas as their comfort level allows.

5. Some questions may be more difficult to answer than others. If you ask a question and no one responds, begin the discussion by venturing an answer yourself. Then ask for comments and other answers. Remember that some questions may have multiple answers.

6. Ask the question "Why?" or "Why do you believe that?" to help continue a discussion and give it greater depth.

7. Give everyone a chance to talk. Keep the conversation moving. Occasionally you may want to direct a question at a specific person who has been quiet. "Do you have anything to add?" is a good follow-up question to another person. If the topic of conversation gets off track, move ahead by asking the next question in your study guide.

8. Before moving from questions to activities, ask group members if they have any questions that have not been answered. Remember that as a leader, you do not have to know all the answers. Some answers may come from group members. Other answers may even need a bit of research. Your job is to keep the discussion moving and to encourage participation.

9. Review the activity in advance. Feel free to modify it or to create your own activity. Encourage participants to try the "At home" activity.

10. Following the conclusion of the activity, close with a brief prayer, praying either the printed prayer from the study guide or a prayer of your own. If your group desires, pause for individual prayer petitions.

11. Be grateful and supportive. Thank group members for their ideas and participation.

12. You are not expected to be a "perfect" leader. Just do the best you can by focusing on the participants and the lesson. God will help you lead this group.

13. Enjoy your time together!

SUGGESTIONS FOR PARTICIPANTS

1. What you will receive from this study will be in direct proportion to your involvement. Be an active participant!

2. Please make a point to attend all sessions and to arrive on time so that you can receive the greatest benefit.

3. Read the chapter and review the study-guide questions prior to the meeting. You may want to jot down questions you have from the reading and also answers to some of the study-guide questions.

4. Be supportive and appreciative of your group leader as well as the other members of your group. You are on a journey together.

5. Your participation is encouraged. Feel free to share your thoughts about the material being discussed.

6. Pray for your group and your leader.

CHAPTER 1

LONELINESS IS A PRIVATE TUTOR...

Snapshot Summary
This first chapter explores loneliness and shows what this instructor can teach us about life, others, and ourselves.

Discussion Questions
1. What insights did you receive from this chapter?
2. How does modern life accentuate loneliness?
3. During Creation, how did God help man fight loneliness? Why do you think God created loneliness in the first place?
4. Recall a time in your life when you were lonely. Why did loneliness come about, and how did you feel?
5. How does sin lead to loneliness?
6. What life lessons can we learn from loneliness?
7. What happens when we suppress loneliness?
8. What are some of the causes of loneliness?
9. When we are lonely, what are we seeking? Fully explain your answer.
10. How do we sometimes cause loneliness for ourselves and for others?

Activities
As a group: Brainstorm ideas on how people can minister to people who are lonely.

At home: Spend some time this week with someone you know who may be lonely.

*Prayer: **Dear God, thank you for giving us loneliness to teach us more about ourselves and about others. Help us to bring our loneliness to you and to remember that we are never alone. You are always with us. Amen.***

148

CHAPTER 2

FRIENDSHIP IS THE LOVELIEST TEACHER...

Snapshot Summary

This chapter looks at friendships and the lessons learned through our relationships with others.

Discussion Questions

1. What insights did you receive from this chapter?
2. How do you define *friendship*?
3. Name some of the various types of friendships.
4. What are some of the risks of friendship?
5. In what ways are friendships a gift from God?
6. Recall a friendship that enriched your life. How did it begin?
7. What causes friendships to thrive?
8. Who was your first childhood friend? What did you and your friend have in common?
9. What causes friendships to fade or to fail?
10. What simple lessons do we learn from friendship?

Activities

As a group: Share the qualities you look for and value in a friendship.

At home: Make an attempt this week to begin a new friendship or to enliven a current one.

Prayer: Dear God, we thank you for our friends and for the meaning and support they give to our lives. Help us to be true friends to others, just as you are a true friend to us. Amen.

CHAPTER 3

DON'T SEEK PAIN...

Snapshot Summary
This chapter helps us to understand pain and shows us what we can learn from it.

Discussion Questions
1. What insights did you receive from this chapter?
2. How do you define *pain?*
3. How can pain be a blessing?
4. Recall a time of pain in your life and the end results.
5. What lessons have you learned from pain?
6. What, if anything, can we do to prevent pain?
7. What does God want us to do with our pain?
8. What does it mean to embrace pain?
9. How is pain or affliction a great equalizer?
10. How can we help our friends and family deal with pain?

Activities
As a group: Discuss different types of pain and the impact that they have on our lives.
At home: Reflect on pain and how it has touched your life. Pray for those in pain.

*Prayer: **Dear God, help us to learn from pain and to learn how to deal with it. Give strength to those in pain, and help us remember that you are with us always. Amen.***

CHAPTER 4

REGRET IS A HUMANIZING TEACHER...

Snapshot Summary
This chapter explores regret, how it shapes our lives, and what it teaches us about ourselves and about others.

Discussion Questions
1. What insights did you receive from this chapter?
2. Share a regret that you have and how it has affected you.
3. What causes us to feel regret?
4. What determines whether regret destroys or refines us?
5. What are some of the things we learn from regret?
6. What is effective or "good" regret? Where should regret lead us?
7. Compare good regret and destructive regret.
8. How is regret an instructive warning?
9. Share how you deal with your regrets. Do you deal with regrets differently now than when you were younger? Explain.
10. What does regret have to do with God's grace?

Activities
As a group: Discuss how regret is a distinguishing human characteristic.
At home: Meditate on regret and on God's grace with our repentance.

Prayer: **Dear God, we have many regrets about what we have done and what we have not done. Help us to learn from these regrets and to deal with them in a constructive manner. Thank you for your grace and forgiveness. Amen.**

CHAPTER 5

LOVE IS A BEAUTIFUL TEACHER...

Snapshot Summary
This chapter explores the many mysteries of love and shows us how we learn from this beautiful instructor.

Discussion Questions
1. What insights did you receive from this chapter?
2. What was the first thing you learned about love?
3. How does love teach us about responsibility?
4. What is the difference between romance and love?
5. What are some of the costs or prices of love?
6. Why do we need to pass love along to others?
7. What person has taught you the most about love? Explain.
8. What are your reflections on the story of Naomi and Ruth?
9. What do you think is the most difficult lesson to learn about love?
10. Explain this statement: "Love is sometimes late, but never too late."

Activities
As a group: Use the Bible (and a Bible commentary, if one is available) to identify and reflect on some passages that teach us about love.

At home: Make an effort to pass love along to someone this week.

Prayer: **Dear God, you are the greatest giver of love. Show us how to love others and ourselves. Thank you for your perfect love. Amen.**

CHAPTER 6

ONLY THE TOUGH LEARN FROM SORROW...

Snapshot Summary
This chapter explores sorrow and shows us some of the tough lessons it teaches.

Discussion Questions
1. What insights did you receive from this chapter?
2. What is your definition of *sorrow*?
3. Why do we need to be tough in order to learn from sorrow?
4. What was one of your first lessons from sorrow?
5. What impresses you about David's experience with sorrow?
6. Why is sorrow inevitable?
7. What are some common causes of sorrow?
8. What are some common reactions to sorrow?
9. How does a person recover from sorrow? Name and describe some strategies.
10. What does God want us to learn from sorrow?

Activities
As a group: Discuss David's experience with sorrow, beginning with the cause and how he dealt with it.

At home: Pray for someone who is dealing with sorrow and, if possible, offer to the person additional meaningful actions of support.

Prayer: Dear God, you know our joys and our sorrows. Help us to learn from our sorrow, and may we remember that you are always with us. Amen.

CHAPTER 7

12-16-07

SIN CAN BE A PRODUCTIVE COURSE...

Snapshot Summary

This chapter deals with sin, a tricky teacher that shows us the wrong way of living but always gives us a choice between good and evil.

Discussion Questions
1. What insights did you receive from this chapter?
2. Recall a lesson you learned from sin.
3. According to the author, how does sin begin? Describe the process.
4. What is the object of sin? What does it want us to do?
5. What are your reflections on the story of Cain and Abel?
6. How is sin a patient teacher?
7. Explain this statement: "Sin is a creature that grows."
8. Explain this statement: "Sin is a master of excuses."
9. What determines whether we learn from sin or do not?
10. How can we win against sin?

Activities

As a group: Discuss what makes us susceptible to sin. List practical strategies for learning from and winning over sin.

At home: Be aware of sin and temptations this week. Keep a mental note of battles won and lost.

*Prayer: **Dear God, we struggle daily with sin. Thank you for your strength, which gives us the power to do what is right. Amen.***

154

CHAPTER 8

SUCCESS IS A FUN COURSE...

Snapshot Summary

This chapter helps us to better understand issues of success and shows us why success needs to be handled with care.

Discussion Questions

1. What insights did you receive from this chapter?
2. How does the world measure success? How do Christians measure it?
3. In your own words, tell what *success* means to you.
4. Recall a success in your life.
5. Talk about someone you know who you feel is a success.
6. Why do we sometimes fail to learn anything from success?
7. Why is gratitude such an important element of success?
8. What is the role of "remembering" when it comes to success?
9. What are some of the hazards of success? What role does humility play in success?
10. Explain this statement: "The problem with success *is* success."

Activities

As a group: Ask each participant to name a successful person and to explain why that person is successful, naming the successful traits that he or she possesses.

At home: Meditate this week on what *success* means to you. Evaluate your strengths and weaknesses, and work on a plan for achieving success.

Prayer: **Dear God, you are the ultimate source of success and meaning in life. Thank you for our small victories and successes. Help us to remember that everything good comes from you. Amen.**

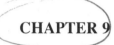

CHAPTER 9

1/20/08
27

DEFEAT IS A REQUIRED COURSE...

Snapshot Summary

This chapter looks at defeat and provides some strategies for learning from it.

Discussion Questions

1. What insights did you receive from this chapter?
2. Recall a defeat from your childhood. How did it happen? How did you feel? How did you handle the situation?
3. What defeats, do you think, are the worst?
4. What is the Christian attitude toward defeat?
5. What are some strategies for dealing with defeat and learning from it?
6. How do you normally react to defeat?
7. What is needed in order to learn from defeat?
8. What causes us to be depressed or angry after a defeat?
9. Why do some people fail to learn from defeat?
10. Is there ever a reason for blame after a defeat? Why or why not? Why do we often place blame?

Activities

As a group: Look in the sports section of a newspaper for comments by players and coaches as to why their team was defeated and discuss these comments. Or cite exam-

156

ples of defeat within your local, national, or world community; and talk about what was or could have been learned by the persons involved and by others.

At home: Make a point to learn from defeat during this coming week. Treat defeat as a teacher.

Prayer: **Dear God, we thank you for being with us in the midst of our defeats. Help us to learn from them and to remember that you give us enough strength to deal with all our disappointments. Amen.**

CHAPTER 10

YOU CAN LEARN FROM YOUR ENEMIES...

Snapshot Summary
This chapter examines how our enemies shape our lives and what we can learn from them.

Discussion Questions
1. What insights did you receive from this chapter?
2. Recall an enemy from your childhood. How did you deal with this person?
3. What are some things we can learn from our enemies?
4. How are enemies created?
5. What happens when we love our enemy?
6. How is prayer a powerful tool against our enemies?
7. How do enemies sometimes change us for the worse?
8. What are some of the positive effects our enemies can have on us?
9. What are personal, inner enemies, and how should we deal with them?
10. How does God want us to handle our enemies?

157

Activities

As a group: Use a current newspaper or magazine to find examples of enemies or adversarial relationships. Discuss what can be learned from them.

At home: Make a list of your inner enemies, and write down some ideas for how you can deal with them.

Prayer: **Dear God, help us to learn from and pray for our enemies. May we remember that your love is within us and how you provide strength for all our challenges. Amen.**

CHAPTER 11

PEOPLE ARE TUITION-FREE COURSES...

Snapshot Summary

This chapter looks at our experiences and relationships with other people and how we learn from them.

Discussion Questions

1. What insights did you receive from this chapter?
2. Give an example of someone you know who taught you a valuable lesson.
3. What part does humility play in learning from other people?
4. What impressed you about the story of Moses?
5. What does it take to be able to learn from another person? What type of student must we be?
6. What are some of the barriers that hold us back from learning from others?
7. Why are some people easier to learn from than others?
8. How do we learn from another person's failure?

9. Why must we be discerning in what we learn from others?
10. In what ways are all of us teachers to other people?

Activities

As a group: Discuss the different ways in which we learn from people. Give examples from your own life.

At home: During the coming week, look for ways in which to learn from other people. Later, recall the things you have learned and reflect on how you can apply this new knowledge in your life.

*Prayer: **Dear God, you have surrounded us with people of all types and personalities. Thank you for the gift of differences in that we are not all alike. May we learn from others as we serve you. Amen.***

CHAPTER 12

YOU CAN LEARN FROM DEATH . . .

Snapshot Summary

This chapter explores death as a teacher to us and shows us how we can learn from it.

Discussion Questions
1. What insights did you receive from this chapter?
2. For what reasons should we learn about death?
3. What death of a family member or friend taught you the most about death?
4. What are the three ways in which we can study death?
5. How has your view of death changed over the years?

6. What are some ways in which we can prepare for death?
7. In what ways is death a blessed servant?
8. How does death affect our relationships with other people?
9. How should death influence the way we live?
10. Is it possible to learn how to die? Explain.

Activities

As a group: Look up hymns in a church hymnal that are commonly used during funerals. What do the words of the hymns tell us about life and death?

At home: Take a walk through a cemetery or another quiet place of reflection this week and meditate on life and death.

Prayer: **Dear God, we thank you that you are with us in life and in death. Be with us as we continue to experience your gift of life. Amen.**